Super Easy and Delicious
AIR FRYER RECIPES

Super Easy and Delicious
AIR FRYER RECIPES

Nutritious and Delicious Ways to Cook Your Favorite Food with Your Air Fryer

············
EMILY PASTER
············

NEW SHOE PRESS

Inspiring | Educating | Creating | Entertaining

First Published in 2023 by New Shoe Press, an imprint of The Quarto Group, 100 Cummings Center, Suite 265-D, Beverly, MA 01915, USA.
T (978) 282-9590 F (978) 283-2742 Quarto.com

New Shoe Press titles are also available at discount for retail, wholesale, promotional, and bulk purchase. For details, contact the Special Sales Manager by email at specialsales@quarto.com or by mail at The Quarto Group, Attn: Special Sales Manager, 100 Cummings Center, Suite 265-D, Beverly, MA 01915, USA.

ISBN: 978-0-7603-8354-4
eISBN: 978-0-7603-8355-1

The content in this book was previously published in *Epic Air Fryer Cookbook* (Harvard Common Press 2020) by Emily Paster.

Library of Congress Cataloging-in-Publication Data available

Photography: Leigh Olson

This one is for Elliot,
who believed I could do it.

Contents

Introduction
Elevate Your Air Frying   8

Chapter 1
Breakfast and Brunch   23

Chapter 2
Appetizers, Snacks, and Party Foods   35

Chapter 3
Vegetarian Main Courses   69

Chapter 4
Chicken, Turkey, and Duck   83
Beef, Lamb, and Pork   97
Seafood   111

Chapter 5
Desserts   125

About the Author   140

Acknowledgments   141

Index   142

Spicy Maple-Soy Brussels Sprouts
p62

Elevate Your Air Frying

If you are reading this book, it is likely because you have purchased, received, or are considering purchasing an air fryer. You are certainly not alone. Air fryers have become one of the hottest kitchen gifts for Christmas, Mother's Day, and even Father's Day. (Although my evidence for that last one is mostly anecdotal, I can say with certainty that men are seriously into the air fryer.) Some say that air fryers have replaced the Instant Pot, and other electric pressure cookers, as the current must-have kitchen appliance.

Why all the commotion about air fryers? My guess is that it is because air fryers have promised to do the impossible: deliver the deep-fried taste of our favorite treats—from french fries to doughnuts—without the mess, bother, and, yes, fat. I know I would happily shell out my hard-earned money for a machine that could make fried chicken and churros—okay, especially churros—healthy.

But a desire to enjoy restaurant-style fried foods at home without oil splattering everywhere—let alone all those calories—is not enough to explain the growing popularity of the air fryer. No one wants to eat that much fried food. While many people may have initially bought their air fryers to make taquitos and fried shrimp, they have quickly learned that the air fryer can do so much more. In fact, I would argue that the air fryer is a new and especially effective ally in the fight to make cooking at home more accessible and convenient for busy families.

As a cookbook author and food blogger, my goal has always been to help people feel confident in the kitchen and inspire them to cook more often for their friends and family. As the author Michael Pollan has written, cooking our own food—instead of relying on restaurants, takeout, and convenience foods—is one of the very best things we can do for our health. Cooking also can be deeply satisfying: it requires us to use our hands to make something tangible from start to finish—an activity that is lacking in our contemporary, digital world. And it is a way to nurture and care for the ones we love.

But as the working mother of two teenagers, both of whom seem to be involved in countless after-school activities, I am all too aware of how difficult it is to actually cook healthy, satisfying meals on a daily basis. Even I, who cooks for a living, often walk in the door at 6 p.m.—usually after driving my kids all over town—and wonder what to make for dinner that night. Many mornings, I beg my kids to eat something nutritious before leaving for a long day of school and practice only to be told that "breakfast is lame" or "I don't have time."

Shrimp DeJonghe Skewers   p123

Like you, I have tried everything to make dinnertime easier and less stressful. I have prepped meals on the weekend, signed up for expensive meal-kit delivery services, and purchased all the latest gadgets, from slow cookers to the Instant Pot. The Instant Pot has turned out to be genuinely helpful. Its ability to cook certain kinds of foods quickly, namely braises, stews, and grains, and keep them warm for hours has been a lifesaver for those afternoons when I am on the go from 4 to 7 p.m.

But the Instant Pot has its limitations. It does an outstanding job with the foods I just mentioned— anything that cooks in liquid. But if you are looking for something crispy, crunchy, seared, or caramelized, well, look elsewhere. Pressure cookers don't do crispy. But you know what does? The air fryer. In many ways, the air fryer is the yin to the Instant Pot's yang. Air fryers cook food quickly, and they deliver crispy chicken, caramelized vegetables, and seared-on-the-outside, tender-on-the-inside meat and fish.

Because of their small size, air fryers need at most a few minutes to preheat and they won't heat up the whole house, like the oven does, which is a godsend in summer. While you still need your oven to bake the perfect birthday cake and roast a Thanksgiving turkey, when it comes to roasted vegetables and moist, juicy chicken and fish, the air fryer is quicker and arguably even better than the oven every time. Since I began cooking with an air fryer, I have told countless friends—from busy professionals to working parents—that they should consider getting one as well. And no, not just so they can make french fries. So that they can make *dinner*. And breakfast. And yes, even dessert. (Did I mention the churros?)

In this book, you will find recipes for your air fryer that range from those you probably expected— Avocado Fries, Chicken Parmesan, and Chinese Takeout Egg Rolls, for example—to many that may surprise you. Imagine using your air fryer to make Orange-Glazed Duck Breast with Apples, Teriyaki Salmon and Broccoli, or Cumin-Crusted Pork Tenderloin. How about a Roasted Red Pepper and Feta Salad, Pecan-Crusted Tilapia, or Strawberries and Cream Baked Oatmeal? With this book, you truly will discover everything that your air fryer can do, from making quick, protein-packed breakfasts to perfect party appetizers to sophisticated desserts. And, of course, plenty of quick-cooking, healthy, *delicious* dinners.

These are air fryer recipes for the way we want to cook and eat today—with global flavors and ingredients, lots of vegetarian and plant-based options, and nutritious, whole foods. You won't find recipes here that rely on heavily processed ingredients—no doughnuts made from canned biscuit dough, for example—because that is not how I cook. What's more, because the air fryer is so quick and efficient, you do not need to rely on shortcuts to create satisfying and tasty from-scratch meals. Many of the recipes in this book can be on the table in under thirty minutes. Those that take longer—such as the yeast-risen Lemon-Lavender Doughnuts—are perfect projects for weekends and days when you have the time and desire to embark on a more ambitious kitchen project.

Regardless of why you wanted an air fryer, I congratulate you on purchasing or receiving one. I think that you will find this countertop appliance to be more versatile and useful than you ever imagined.

How to Use
Your Air Fryer

What Is an Air Fryer?
How Does It Work?

While I was writing this book, I taught a cooking class—as I do every month—at the Chicago Botanic Garden. During the course of the class, I mentioned that I was working on a cookbook of air fryer recipes, and one of the students said to me with a slight air of exasperation, "Aren't they just *ovens*?" I laughed. It was funny because it was true. When you come right down to it, she was right: your air fryer is a kind of countertop oven. Specifically, it is a powerful countertop convection oven.

Many of us are familiar with convection ovens. The large oven in your kitchen may well have a convection feature that you use or, more likely, don't use. I rarely use the convection feature on my wall oven because I am anxious about having to adjust the cooking time and temperature of the recipe that I am following. Convection ovens have fans and exhaust systems that move the hot air of the oven around the food being baked so that it cooks more quickly and evenly. (Maybe we should start using that convection setting after all.) A convection oven is also drier than a regular oven because the exhaust system whisks away any moisture that has built up in the closed oven, causing foods to become more browned and caramelized.

Tempura Shishito Peppers p60

An air fryer is essentially a small convection oven that gets hotter and moves air faster than other convection ovens. As a result, the air fryer cooks food quickly and does an excellent job of making the exterior dry, browned, and crispy while keeping the interior moist and juicy. When you coat food with a dry breading, or wrap it in pastry, and brush or spray the exterior with oil, the powerful fan circulates the tiny droplets of oil around the food, which mimics, in some ways, the effects of deep-frying.

So the air fryer can mimic the effects of deep-frying, with a small amount of oil. It can also bake and roast certain foods more evenly and in less time than it would take in an oven. What's more, the air fryer whisks away moisture, just like the convection setting on your oven, which allows it essentially to dry out foods with a lot of moisture in them, such as certain vegetables, and make them crispy and caramelized as opposed to soggy. And speaking of soggy, you know how some foods, like pizza, get limp and rubbery when you reheat them in the microwave? The air fryer solves that problem. It actually makes foods crispier upon reheating by whisking away any moisture that has accumulated from storage in the refrigerator.

To sum up, let's review what you can do with your air fryer. First, you can mimic the taste and texture of deep-fried foods—not perfectly, but pretty well—using just teaspoons and tablespoons of oil as opposed to cups. You can also bake and roast meat, fish, and vegetables—again with very little added fat—in less time and sometimes with better results than in the oven. You can reheat foods without making them limp and soggy like a microwave does. And you can do all of this without heating up the whole house and with a portable appliance that can be moved around and brought to rental and vacation homes. That's a lot of functions from one small appliance.

Now that you know what an air fryer is and how it works, let's learn a little more about how to use and care for your air fryer. First, let's discuss the different types of air fryers on the market so you understand how to use the one you own, or how to choose one if you are still in the market.

Profiteroles p132

Kinds of Air Fryers and Choosing the Right Appliance

When air fryers first came on the market, they typically were cylindrical, somewhat like a large egg, with a drawer that pulls out and contains a basket for holding food. Many models, including some of the best-selling ones, still look this way. The machines vary in size, in the capacity of the interior basket—from 2 to almost 6 quarts—and in wattage. The air fryer basket has holes to allow air to circulate and is lined with a nonstick coating to prevent food from sticking. You set the temperature and the cooking time with a dial or, on more advanced models, using a digital display. Some even have preset settings for popular foods, such as frozen chicken nuggets or fries. This model of appliance shuts off automatically when you pull out the drawer to turn or check on the food in the basket and starts up again right away when you push the drawer back in.

Some companies have introduced a new style of air fryer that looks like a large toaster oven and is boxy and rectangular. Some of these machines actually have multiple functions, including toasting, broiling, and regular (i.e., not convection) baking as well as air frying. (The idea, plainly, is that instead of having both a countertop toaster oven *and* an air fryer, you could have one machine to perform all these functions, thereby saving counter space.) These air fryers have a door that opens, just like an oven. These toaster oven–style air fryers have a mesh basket to hold the food that sits above a solid metal tray, which catches any debris that might fall. These models also feature racks that can be adjusted to different heights for different functions.

Although these different models are still air fryers, there are some differences in how they function and how you should approach using them. In general, I have found that the toaster oven–style of air fryer is more powerful than the drawer style. If you have a toaster oven–style appliance, try cooking food at about 25 degrees lower than the suggested temperature of most air fryer recipes and check the food before the end of the recommended cooking time. Also, the holes in the mesh basket of the toaster oven–style machine are typically larger than the holes of the basket in the drawer style, so more debris may fall through to the tray below. (As I explain later, I recommend lining the metal tray under the mesh basket with foil for this reason.)

Lastly, the mesh basket of the toaster oven–style sits closer to the heating element of the air fryer than the basket in the drawer style. As a result, some thicker foods, such as whole chicken breasts or bell peppers, may not fit in the tray without touching the heating element, which will cause scorching. You will have to cut or trim these foods as needed to avoid this. (I will indicate in specific recipes where this problem arises.)

So which air fryer should you purchase? If you are reading this book, chances are that you already own an air fryer. But it is possible that some readers are still trying to decide whether to get an air fryer—I think I have made a pretty compelling case there. And, if so, which one to get. The most important factor to consider when choosing an air fryer is size. (Yes, size does matter.) There is the size of the appliance itself—that is, how much room it takes up on your counter and how heavy it is—and also the capacity of the basket. As I will explain, it is important not to overcrowd the basket of the air fryer, which means that sometimes you have to cook food in batches. If you have a small air fryer and are cooking for a large group, this can add a lot of time to your meal preparation. A small machine with a 3-quart basket is okay if you are usually cooking for only 1 or 2 people. If you are usually cooking for 3 or more people, however, I highly recommend a bigger model with a basket of 5 quarts or larger. The toaster oven–style air fryer takes up more room on your counter, but it also has a larger capacity, which makes cooking quicker and more efficient, so that is another factor to consider.

Beyond size and cooking capacity, there is not much difference between air fryers in terms of how well they cook food. The other differences—and what causes some models to be more expensive than others—are mostly a matter of convenience and style. Less expensive models often feature dials for temperature and cooking time. Higher-end models have digital displays that allow you to choose the precise cooking temperature and time. Some models are noisier than others, and some have more parts and are harder to clean.

My advice when choosing an air fryer is to consider how your family will use it. How many people are you usually cooking for? Will the air fryer live on the counter? If so, consider how much counter space you have, keeping in mind that the air fryer needs 5 inches (13 cm) of clearance on all sides. (More on that in a bit.) Will the air fryer live in a closet and need to be brought out every time you want to use it? In that case, check the weight of the different models. Then, once you know the size you want, decide on a budget. You can easily spend anywhere from $50 to $300 on an air fryer. Research the different models in your price range and read plenty of reviews before making the final decision.

Tips on Using Your Air Fryer

When using your air fryer, there are a few general principles to follow to ensure that you get deliciously consistent results:

Don't Overfill the Basket

As I mentioned before, the air fryer fan blows hot air around the food in the basket, which causes browning and caramelization. Therefore, it is important not to crowd the basket with too much food, which would prevent the air from circulating—even if that means having to cook food in two or sometimes three batches. If you overfill the basket, the food will steam instead of baking or roasting. Steamed food is limp and soggy, not brown and crispy. It is also important not to cover or line the air fryer basket with foil or parchment paper—unless the parchment paper also has holes or perforations—except in very rare instances. Also, be sure to flip or turn the food during cooking to make sure that all sides are exposed to the hot air. (I usually indicate in the recipes how often and when to turn food.)

Dry Batter, Not Wet

When you think about fried foods, you may imagine foods coated with a wet batter such as tempura or a beer batter. These wet batters work well when deep-frying but not in the air fryer. The powerful fan could easily blow the batter off the food and create quite a mess inside your machine. In general, stick with a dry coating, such as flour, cornstarch, or bread crumbs. Many of the "fried" recipes in this book call for you to coat food in flour, then dip it in an egg wash, and then, finally, coat it with dry bread crumbs, especially

Japanese panko bread crumbs, which are exceptionally light and crispy. Following this three-part process, which you will notice throughout the book, will help the coating stick to your food and make the food's exterior as crunchy and crispy as if it were deep-fried.

Use a Little Bit of Oil (But Not EVOO)

You may have hoped to make fried foods with no oil at all in the air fryer. But you will not end up with deliciously browned and crisp foods without at least some added fat. Also, spraying the basket of the air fryer with oil prevents certain foods from sticking. For foods that you have coated with flour, bread crumbs, or other dry coatings, spray them with oil right before cooking them in the air fryer. For foods like potatoes, vegetables, and lean meats, such as chicken without skin, brush or toss them with a little bit of oil—anywhere from a few teaspoons to a tablespoon—right before cooking. (In other words, do not oil foods in advance.) For foods that are naturally fatty, such as red meat or skin-on chicken, there is no need to add additional oil. Although I love extra-virgin olive oil for sautéing foods on the stove and for making salad dressing, I do not recommend it for cooking foods in the air fryer except where specified. Extra-virgin olive oil has a low smoke point, and the air fryer cooks foods at high temperatures. I recommend instead a neutral-tasting oil with a high smoke point such as vegetable, canola, or grapeseed. (Where the recipes ask for vegetable oil, feel free to substitute canola or grapeseed.)

Preheat. Don't Overcook

Remember when I told you that the air fryer does not need to preheat, unlike your regular oven? That wasn't entirely true. When using your large oven, it is absolutely essential that you let it come up to temperature before putting food in it. And that can sometimes take ten or even twenty minutes. When using your air fryer, it is helpful if you preheat it before using, but just a few minutes of preheating are necessary. And sometimes it doesn't even need that. When I think a dish will come out significantly better if you preheat the air fryer first, I will indicate that in the recipe. On a related note, the air fryer cooks food very quickly, and remember that the fan dries food out. Be sure to watch your food carefully to prevent burning and overcooking, which could make your food dry and tough. Do not hesitate to open the drawer to check on food while it cooks, especially when you are first using your air fryer and learning how it works.

Accessories

Don't you hate it when you buy an expensive new kitchen appliance only to discover that you now have to buy a bunch of accessories to use it? The good news is that the only accessory you really must purchase to get the most out of your air fryer is an oil sprayer or mister. As I explain previously, spraying breaded foods with oil is essential to achieving a crispy, crunchy, deep-fried texture, *and* using store-bought cooking sprays with propellants and other chemicals can damage the nonstick coating of the air fryer basket. The solution to this dilemma is to buy a refillable oil sprayer or mister that will allow you to spray your food with oil and nothing else. I recommend purchasing one specifically designed to spray oil because oil can clog the nozzle of a regular spray bottle. (In the interest of full disclosure, even the sprayers designed for oil have a tendency to clog and stop working as well after a while because oil is so viscous.) Beyond the oil mister, there are a few additional accessories that you may want to invest in. A small cake or pizza pan that fits inside your air fryer will be helpful to make some of the breakfast and dessert recipes in this book like the Speedy Shakshuka and the Roasted Strawberry Tart with Honey and Balsamic Vinegar. And because regular skewers are too long to fit in most air fryers, you may also want a set of metal skewers specially designed for your machine. There are many air fryer accessory kits on the market that have pans, skewers, and more for a reasonable price. One last kitchen accessory that I recommend for everyone is a reliable, instant-read thermometer to make sure that you are cooking meat, fish, and chicken to a safe internal temperature.

Safety and Caring for Your Air Fryer

Now that you understand how the air fryer works and the different models that are available, you may be wondering how to use yours safely and how to protect your investment. The good news is that air fryers are exceptionally easy to use right out of the box. However, there are some important safety considerations and tricks that will help you take care of your appliance. First, understand that the air fryer gets quite hot. Be sure to set yours up on a stable, heat-proof surface. It is not a bad idea to invest in a heat-resistant mat to place under the air fryer to protect your countertops. And when you remove the drawer containing the basket, always set it down on a heat-resistant surface as well. (Treat it like a hot pot coming off the stove, essentially.)

Also, because air fryers are equipped with an exhaust system, air needs to be able to circulate around the machine. In other words, do not place it right up against the backsplash or next to another object. Allow at least 5 inches (13 cm) of space on all sides. (Because of that exhaust system, air fryers can be loud. You will certainly notice the noise of the fan blowing when it is in use.) Keep your hands and face away from the vents, which may release hot air or steam during the cooking cycle.

It is important for the longevity of your machine to take care with the nonstick coating lining the basket. If it starts to chip or wear off, food will stick to the basket and it will not work as well. (You may also be concerned about particles of the nonstick coating getting into your food.) To that end, only use nonstick-safe utensils, such as those made of silicone, to remove food from the basket. Avoid metal utensils. Also, avoid using store-bought cooking sprays. These sprays contain propellants that can harm the basket's nonstick coating. Instead, invest in a mister or sprayer that you fill with oil. Use this and only this to spray oil onto foods prior to air frying. I will talk more about oil misters a bit later when I discuss accessories for your air fryer. (Depending on the food, you can also brush it with oil using a pastry brush.)

You should clean your air fryer after each use—once it is cool enough to handle, of course. If you do not clean the basket or mesh tray frequently, leftover food particles and residue can affect the taste of your food. When cleaning any part of your air fryer, do not use harsh cleansers or rough scrubbing surfaces. A sponge, soap, and water are best. For a drawer-style model, pull out the drawer and remove the basket. Wash it with soap and water. If food has stuck to the basket, soak it until the food can be easily washed off. Oil, batter, or even food particles may fall to the bottom of the drawer. Dump out any food particles and wipe the bottom with a damp cloth or sponge to remove debris that is caked on. For toaster oven–style models, I recommend lining the metal baking tray under the mesh basket with foil for easier cleanup. Change the foil when it gets dirty and wash the tray regularly. As for the mesh basket itself, wash it with soap and water after each use, soaking it first as necessary.

A Note on Salt

Salt is one of the most important ingredients in all of cooking. Whenever I call for salt in this book, I mean a coarse salt like kosher salt or coarse sea salt, not table salt, which is iodized to prevent clumping. The larger size of kosher salt is ideal for drawing moisture out of meat and vegetables without making your food taste overly salty, and because it has no added ingredients, it has a cleaner taste. If you are using table salt, use half of the amount that I call for in the recipe and add more if needed.

In addition, season food with salt as you go. When sautéing, for example, season an ingredient with salt as soon as you add it to the pan. This will not only help build flavor but it will help the food cook better by drawing out moisture. Season meats with salt and pepper prior to cooking. Many sweet recipes call for a pinch of salt; this will not make your baked goods taste salty, I promise. It merely helps enhance flavor. You may also want to add a flaky sea salt, such as Maldon, to your pantry and use it to sprinkle on finished dishes. You want those crispy fries and juicy meats to burst with flavor.

CHAPTER 1
Breakfast and Brunch

Speedy Shakshuka   24

Asparagus and Goat Cheese Frittata   25

Freeze-and-Fry Sweet Potato and Black Bean
Breakfast Burritos   26

Eggs in a Basket   28

Cinnamon Streusel French Toast   29

Apple Fritters   30

Two-Ingredient Cream Biscuits   32

Strawberries and Cream Baked Oatmeal   33

Speedy Shakshuka

Shakshuka is a North African dish that is a popular breakfast in Israel. Lately, I have noticed it appearing on American restaurant brunch menus, and with good reason. Shakshuka—which is nothing more than eggs poached in a spicy tomato and pepper sauce—is healthy, satisfying, and will jump-start your day with a spicy kick. It also is easy to make at home.

The most time-consuming part of this recipe is the tomato and pepper sauce. Happily, you can make the sauce in advance, and this recipe makes enough for multiple batches of shakshuka. (If you are really pressed for time, you can also use your favorite spicy, store-bought tomato sauce.) If you have the sauce on hand, you can prepare this shakshuka in under fifteen minutes and serve your family a quick, tasty breakfast that is packed with protein and vegetables.

TOMATO SAUCE

3 tablespoons (45 ml) extra-virgin olive oil

1 small yellow onion, diced

1 jalapeño pepper, seeded and minced

1 red bell pepper, diced

2 cloves garlic, minced

1 teaspoon cumin

1 teaspoon sweet paprika

Pinch cayenne pepper

1 tablespoon (16 g) tomato paste

1 can (28 ounces, or 800 g) whole plum tomatoes with juice

2 teaspoons granulated sugar

SHAKSHUKA

4 eggs

1 tablespoon (15 ml) heavy cream

1 tablespoon (1 g) chopped cilantro

Kosher salt and pepper to taste

—

Serves 2

Heat the olive oil in a large, deep skillet over medium heat. Add the onion and peppers, season with salt, and sauté until softened, about 10 minutes. Add the garlic and spices and sauté a few additional minutes until fragrant. Add the tomato paste and stir to combine. Add the plum tomatoes along with their juice—breaking up the tomatoes with a spoon—and the sugar. Turn the heat to high and bring the mixture to a boil. Turn the heat down and simmer until the tomatoes are thickened, about 10 minutes. Turn off the heat. (May be done in advance. Refrigerate the sauce if not using right away.)

Crack the eggs into a 7-inch (18 cm) round cake pan insert for the air fryer. Remove 1 cup of the tomato sauce from the skillet and spoon it over the egg whites only, leaving the yolks exposed. Drizzle the cream over the yolks.

Place the cake pan in the air fryer and cook at 300°F (150°C) for 10 to 12 minutes, until the egg whites are set and the yolks still runny. Remove the pan from the air fryer and garnish with chopped cilantro. Season with salt and pepper.

Serve immediately with crusty bread to mop up the sauce.

Asparagus and Goat Cheese Frittata

A frittata is an example of an egg dish that takes a long time to cook in the oven and therefore has, up to now, been reserved for weekend mornings and brunch. No more! In the air fryer, you can make a fluffy, elegant frittata—filled with your favorite vegetables—in just twenty minutes using very little oil or butter. Frittatas may just become your new favorite weekday breakfast.

The combination of asparagus and goat cheese is a classic. But I encourage you to experiment with different vegetables, herbs, and cheeses as the seasons change. Cooking the vegetables alone for a few minutes before pouring in the egg mixture ensures that they will come out tender.

1 cup (134 g) asparagus spears, cut into 1-inch (2.5 cm) pieces

1 teaspoon vegetable oil

6 eggs

1 tablespoon (15 ml) milk

2 ounces (55 g) goat cheese

1 tablespoon (3 g) minced chives (optional)

Kosher salt and pepper

—

Serves 2 to 4

Toss the asparagus pieces with the vegetable oil in a small bowl. Place the asparagus in a 7-inch (18 cm) round air fryer cake pan insert and place the pan in the air fryer. Cook at 400°F (200°C) for 5 minutes until the asparagus is softened and slightly wrinkled. Remove the pan.

Whisk together the eggs and milk and pour the mixture over the asparagus in the pan. Crumble the goat cheese over the top of the eggs and add the chives, if using. Season with a pinch of salt and pepper. Return the pan to the air fryer and bake at 320°F (160°C) for 20 minutes, until the eggs are set and cooked through. Serve immediately.

Freeze-and-Fry Sweet Potato and Black Bean Breakfast Burritos

Breakfast burritos are a grab-and-go, weekday morning favorite. The frozen, store-bought versions can be expensive and full of unfamiliar ingredients. Save money and eat healthier by making a batch of these easy breakfast burritos over the weekend and freezing them. When you wake up in the morning, pop one of the burritos into the air fryer to heat while you get ready. They only need 20 minutes to go from freezer to warm, cheesy, and ready to eat. For a crispy outside, like a chimichanga, brush the burrito with oil and heat for an additional 5 minutes.

With refried black beans, roasted sweet potatoes—also cooked in the air fryer—spinach, scrambled eggs, and just a sprinkle of cheese, these breakfast burritos are full of vitamins and protein and will satisfy even the hungriest appetite until lunchtime.

2 sweet potatoes, peeled and cut into a small dice

1 tablespoon (15 ml) vegetable oil

Kosher salt and pepper to taste

6 large flour tortillas

1 can (16 ounces, or 455 g) refried black beans, divided

1½ cups (45 g) baby spinach, lightly packed, divided

6 eggs, scrambled

¾ cup (90 g) grated Cheddar or Monterey Jack cheese, divided

Vegetable oil for heating

Salsa, Roasted Garlic Guacamole (page 50), and sour cream (optional)

—

Makes 6 burritos

Toss the sweet potatoes with the vegetable oil, season with salt and pepper, and cook in the air fryer at 400°F (200°C) until cooked through, about 10 minutes. Remove and set aside.

Take a flour tortilla and spread ¼ cup (59.5 g) of the refried beans down the center, leaving a border at each end. Top with ¼ cup (8 g) of the spinach leaves. Sprinkle ¼ cup (27.5 g) plus 2 tablespoons (14 g) of sweet potato cubes on top of the spinach. Top with one-sixth of the scrambled eggs and 2 tablespoons grated cheese. To wrap the burrito, fold the long side over the ingredients, then fold in the short sides and roll. Repeat with the remaining ingredients and tortillas.

Wrap each burrito tightly in foil and combine in a large, gallon-size freezer bag. Freeze for up to 3 months.

To heat, place the burrito, still wrapped in foil, in the air fryer and cook at 350°F (180°C) for 20 minutes, flipping once halfway through. Remove the burrito from the foil, brush the outside of the tortilla with 1 teaspoon oil, and heat for an additional 3 to 5 minutes, turning once. Serve with salsa, Roasted Garlic Guacamole (page 50), or sour cream as desired.

Eggs in a Basket

Eggs in a Basket, also known to Americans as Toad in the Hole, is nothing more than a fried egg cooked in a piece of bread. The bread becomes crispy and buttery as it fries along with the egg. As for the egg, it is cooked just until the white is set but the yolk is still runny, so you can mop it up with the crispy, buttery fried bread. No wonder it is my son's favorite breakfast, especially when I make it with a hearty country or Italian bread sliced thick enough to hold the egg in a nice round circle.

The air fryer version of Eggs in a Basket may free me forever from early mornings standing over the stove. Using a cake pan insert for your air fryer, you can bake the egg inside the bread in less than ten minutes. A light coating of melted butter on both sides of the bread creates the same crispy, fried texture as the skillet version but with less fat. This version is so easy, my son can even make it for himself!

1 thick slice country, sourdough, or Italian bread

2 tablespoons (28 g) unsalted butter, melted

1 egg

Kosher salt and pepper to taste

—

Serves 1

Brush the bottom of the air fryer cake pan insert and both sides of the bread with melted butter. Using a small round cookie or biscuit cutter, cut a hole out of the middle of the bread and set it aside.

Place the slice of bread in the air fryer cake pan insert. Crack the egg into the hole in the bread, taking care not to break the yolk. Season with salt and pepper. Place the cut-out bread hole next to the slice of bread. Place the cake pan insert into the air fryer.

Bake at 300°F (150°C) for 6 to 8 minutes until the egg white is set but the yolk is still runny. Using a silicone spatula, remove the bread slice to a plate. Serve with the cut-out bread circle on the side or place it on top of the egg.

Cinnamon Streusel French Toast

The air fryer makes gorgeously browned, crispy French toast, with no oil or butter, in less than ten minutes. Now this weekend breakfast treat can become an everyday favorite! Any white sandwich bread will work, but, for the best flavor, try a rich, eggy bread such as challah or brioche. Slightly stale bread will hold its shape better, so if you plan to make French toast in the morning, leave the bread out the night before.

For extra sweetness and crunch, I like to add a cinnamon streusel topping to my French toast. It's indulgent, sure, but the sweet, buttery taste is irresistible. This recipe makes enough streusel for several batches of French toast. Store it in the freezer until needed. You could even double the recipe and have some on hand whenever the mood for French toast strikes—which, in my experience, is sometimes at dessert time.

STREUSEL

½ cup (63 g) all-purpose flour

¼ cup (50 g) granulated sugar

¼ cup (38 g) light brown sugar

½ teaspoon cinnamon

Pinch kosher salt

4 tablespoons (55 g) unsalted butter, melted

FRENCH TOAST

2 eggs

¼ cup (60 ml) milk

1 teaspoon vanilla extract

½ teaspoon cinnamon

Pinch nutmeg

4 slices brioche, challah, or white bread, preferably slightly stale

Maple syrup for serving

—
Serves 4

To make the streusel, combine the flour, sugars, cinnamon, and salt in a medium bowl. Pour the melted butter over the dry ingredients and stir with a fork to combine. Transfer the mixture to a plastic bag and place it in the freezer while you prepare the French toast. (May be made ahead.)

To make the French toast, whisk together the eggs, milk, vanilla, cinnamon, and nutmeg in a medium bowl. Line the air fryer basket with perforated parchment paper to prevent sticking. Dunk each slice of bread in the egg mixture, making sure both sides are coated. Hold the bread over the bowl for a moment to allow any excess liquid to slide off.

Place the bread in the air fryer basket. Cook at 375°F (190°C) for 5 minutes. Open the air fryer and turn the bread over. Top each slice of bread with 2 tablespoons (40 g) of streusel. Cook for an additional 4 minutes until the bread is crispy and browned and the streusel is puffy and golden. Serve warm with maple syrup.

Apple Fritters

These apple fritters are an old-fashioned sweet breakfast treat that feels as indulgent as a doughnut but without all the fat. Diced apples are folded into a cake-like batter, which is then scooped directly onto the basket of the air fryer and cooked in less than ten minutes. Once the fritters have cooled a bit, you can give them a light glaze or simply dust with powdered sugar.

The batter tends to stick to the basket of the air fryer, so be sure to oil it well or line the basket with perforated parchment paper. Use a thin spatula that is safe for nonstick coating to remove the fritters from the basket.

FRITTERS

2 firm apples, such as Granny Smith, peeled, cored, and diced

Juice from 1 lemon

½ teaspoon cinnamon

1 cup (125 g) all-purpose flour

1½ teaspoons baking powder

½ teaspoon kosher salt

2 tablespoons (26 g) granulated sugar

2 eggs

¼ cup (60 ml) milk

2 tablespoons (28 g) unsalted butter, melted

Vegetable oil for spraying

GLAZE

1¼ cups (125 g) powdered sugar, sifted

½ teaspoon vanilla extract

¼ cup (60 ml) water

—

Makes 15 fritters, to serve 4 or 5

To make the fritters, toss the diced apples with the lemon juice and cinnamon in a small bowl and set aside. In a large bowl, whisk together the flour, baking powder, and salt. In a medium bowl, whisk together the sugar and eggs until the mixture is pale yellow. Whisk in the milk followed by the melted butter. Add the wet ingredients to the dry ingredients in the large bowl and stir to combine. Fold in the diced apples.

Brush the basket of the air fryer with oil or line with perforated parchment paper to prevent sticking. Working in 3 batches and using a spring-loaded cookie scoop, ice cream scoop, or ¼-cup measure, scoop 5 balls of dough directly onto the air fryer basket. Spray the fritters with oil. Cook at 360°F (182°C) for 7 to 8 minutes until the outside is browned and the inside is fully cooked. Remove the cooked fritters to a cooling rack and repeat 2 more times with the remaining dough.

Make the glaze by whisking together the powdered sugar, vanilla, and water in a small bowl. (The glaze should be thin.) Drizzle the glaze over the fritters or dip the tops of the fritters directly in the glaze, letting any excess drip off.

Serve warm.

Two-Ingredient Cream Biscuits

By using your air fryer, you can make tender biscuits with flaky layers in just twenty minutes without heating up the whole house. When it is this easy to make biscuits from scratch, there is no need to buy refrigerated biscuit dough ever again. Serve with butter and honey alongside eggs, sausage, or bacon for an old-fashioned, homestyle breakfast. Needless to say, these biscuits are also delightful at dinnertime to accompany soups and stews.

The secret to this recipe is self-rising flour. Self-rising flour already contains salt and leavening, eliminating the need to sift and measure any additional ingredients. Southern and British cooks rely on it quite a bit in their baking. Self-rising flour is available everywhere, but you can make your own by adding 1½ teaspoons of baking powder and 1/2 teaspoon of salt to 1 cup of all-purpose flour.

1 cup (125 g) self-rising flour

½ cup (120 ml) plus 1 tablespoon (15 ml) heavy cream

Vegetable oil for spraying

2 tablespoons (28 g) unsalted butter, melted (optional)

—

Makes 6 or 7 biscuits

Place the flour in a medium bowl and whisk to remove any lumps. Make a well in the center of the flour. While stirring with a fork, slowly pour in the cream in a steady stream. Continue to stir until the dough has mostly come together. With your hands, gather the dough, incorporating any dry flour, and form it into a ball.

Place the dough on a lightly floured board and pat into a rectangle that is ½ to ¾ inch (1.3 to 2 cm) thick. Fold in half. Turn and repeat. One more time, pat the dough into a ¾-inch-thick (2 cm) rectangle. Using a 2-inch (5 cm) biscuit cutter, cut out biscuits—close together to minimize waste—taking care not to twist the cutter when pulling it up. You should be able to cut out 5 biscuits. Gather up any scraps and cut out 1 or 2 more biscuits. (These may be misshapen and slightly tougher than the first 5 biscuits, but still delicious.)

Preheat the air fryer to 325°F (170°C) for 3 minutes. Spray the air fryer basket with oil to prevent sticking. Place the biscuits in the air fryer basket so that they are barely touching. Cook for 15 to 18 minutes until the tops are browned and the insides fully cooked. Remove the biscuits to a plate, brush the tops with melted butter, if using, and serve.

Strawberries and Cream Baked Oatmeal

Baked oatmeal is another warm, comforting breakfast that cooks up quickly and with very little preparation using the air fryer. With whole grains from the rolled oats and protein from the milk and egg, this baked oatmeal will keep everyone in your family full and satisfied until lunch. And the berries and brown sugar make all that healthy goodness go down easily. The splash of cream makes this version of baked oatmeal taste especially rich, but if you don't have cream on hand, using all milk is fine.

Any fresh berry will work in place of the strawberries. In the summer months, try using sliced stone fruits, such as peaches and nectarines, for a seasonal treat.

1 cup (170 g) sliced strawberries

1 egg

¾ cup (180 ml) milk

¼ cup (60 ml) heavy cream

1 cup (80 g) rolled oats

2 tablespoons (19 g) brown sugar

½ teaspoon baking powder

½ teaspoon cinnamon

½ teaspoon ginger

Pinch salt

1 tablespoon (14 g) unsalted butter (optional)

—

Serves 2 to 4

Place the sliced strawberries in the bottom of the cake pan insert for the air fryer, reserving a few for garnish. In a small bowl, whisk together the egg, milk, and cream and pour it over the strawberries in the pan.

In a small bowl, combine the rolled oats, brown sugar, baking powder, spices, and salt. Add the dry ingredients to the wet ingredients in the cake pan and stir to combine. Allow to rest for 10 minutes. Place the reserved strawberries on top of the oatmeal.

Place the cake pan in the air fryer and bake at 320°F (160°C) for 15 minutes until the oatmeal is warmed through and puffed. Spoon the oatmeal into bowls. If desired, add a pat of butter to each bowl for extra richness.

CHAPTER 2
Appetizers, Snacks, and Party Foods

Potato and Cheese Taquitos — 36

Chorizo Scotch Eggs — 37

Suppli al Telefono (Roman Rice Croquettes) — 38

Orange and Rosemary Roasted Chickpeas — 41

Fried Pickles with Buttermilk-Herb Ranch Dressing — 42

Crispy Vegetable Spring Rolls — 44

Chinese Takeout Egg Rolls with Soy-Vinegar Dipping Sauce — 46

Pork and Cabbage Gyoza — 47

Crab Rangoon — 48

Roasted Garlic Guacamole with Homemade Tortilla Chips — 50

Smoky Eggplant Dip with Homemade Pita Chips — 52

Tandoori Yogurt Dip with Naan Breadsticks — 53

Fried Green Tomatoes with Rémoulade — 54

Low Country Hush Puppies — 55

Elotes (Mexican Street Corn) — 56

Prosciutto-Wrapped Asparagus — 58

Caribbean Yuca Fries — 59

Tempura Shishito Peppers — 60

Spicy Maple-Soy Brussels Sprouts — 62

Sweet and Smoky Candied Pecans — 63

Avocado Fries with Pomegranate Molasses — 64

KFC (Korean Fried Cauliflower) — 66

Roasted Red Pepper and Feta Salad — 67

Potato and Cheese Taquitos

This is a vegetarian version of taquitos using mashed potato as the filling. Known as *taquitos dorados de papa*, these are quite popular in Mexico. The crispy tortilla contrasts beautifully with the creamy mashed potato and cheese filling, which gets hot and gooey in the air fryer.

These vegetarian taquitos are a sublime way to repurpose leftover mashed potatoes. If you don't have any mashed potatoes on hand and you simply *must* have these mashed potato taquitos, it is easy to make a small batch. Peel and chop 1½ pounds (680 g) potatoes and cook them in boiling salted water until soft. Mash with butter and a splash of warm milk and proceed with the recipe.

2 cups (450 g) mashed potatoes

½ cup (58 g) shredded Mexican cheese

12 corn tortillas

Vegetable oil for spraying

Shredded lettuce, chopped cilantro, pico de gallo, Roasted Garlic Guacamole (page 50), or sour cream for serving

—

Makes 12 taquitos or 4 to 6 servings

Mix the mashed potatoes and cheese in a bowl until thoroughly combined. Soften the tortillas by wrapping them, 1 or 2 at a time, in a damp paper towel and microwaving them on high for 30 seconds.

Place 3 tablespoons (42 g) of the potato-cheese mixture down the middle of a softened tortilla. Roll it closed and secure it with 2 toothpicks. Place the filled tortilla on a lined baking sheet. Repeat with the remaining tortillas.

Spray the outside of each tortilla with a light coating of oil. Place up to 4 tortillas in the basket of the air fryer and cook at 400°F (200°C) for 6 minutes, flipping once halfway through. Repeat with the remaining tortillas.

Serve immediately, garnished with shredded lettuce, chopped cilantro and pico de gallo, Roasted Garlic Guacamole (page 50), or sour cream.

Chorizo Scotch Eggs

The English sure do love their pub grub. Take the Scotch egg, which has been around since the 1700s. A hard-boiled egg wrapped in sausage meat then breaded and deep-fried *does* make an excellent accompaniment to a pint of ale, so I guess those Brits know what they are talking about!

I have updated the classic Scotch egg by starting with a soft-boiled egg, complete with a jammy yolk, and wrapping it in Mexican chorizo for extra flavor. Mexican chorizo is a spicy, uncooked ground meat sausage. It is usually sold loose, not in casings, which is what you want here. Scotch eggs will never be diet food, but when you cook them in the air fryer instead of deep-frying them, they are at least marginally better for you. And just as good with a pint of ale.

1 pound (455 g) Mexican chorizo or other seasoned sausage meat

4 soft-boiled eggs plus 1 raw egg

½ cup (63 g) all-purpose flour

1 cup (50 g) panko bread crumbs

Vegetable oil for spraying

—
Makes 4 eggs

Divide the chorizo into 4 equal portions. Flatten each portion into a disc. Place a soft-boiled egg in the center of each disc. Wrap the chorizo around the egg, encasing it completely. Place the encased eggs on a plate and chill for at least 30 minutes.

Beat the raw egg with 1 tablespoon (15 ml) of water. Place the flour on a small plate and the panko on a second plate. Working with 1 egg at a time, roll the encased egg in the flour, then dip it in the egg mixture. Dredge the egg in the panko and place on a plate. Repeat with the remaining eggs.

Spray the eggs with oil and place in the basket of the air fryer. Cook at 360°F (182°C) for 10 minutes. Turn and cook an additional 5 to 10 minutes until browned and crisp on all sides. Serve immediately.

Supplì al Telefono
(Roman Rice Croquettes)

This Roman bar snack's adorable name may soon be outdated. When you break open one of these fried rice croquettes, the mozzarella in the center stretches long and thin—just like an old-fashioned telephone cord. Hence *supplì al telefono*. No one has phones with cords anymore, but the cheese-pull on these supplì is nothing short of epic.

Supplì were intended as a use for leftover risotto. They are so tasty, however, that it is worth making a batch of risotto for no other purpose than to make it into these rice balls. You can also use leftover short-grain rice other than risotto, such as sushi rice.

RICE CROQUETTES

3½ cups (840 ml) chicken or vegetable stock

4 tablespoons (55 g) unsalted butter

1 small yellow onion, minced

1 cup (195 g) Arborio rice

½ cup (120 ml) dry white wine

½ cup (50 g) grated Parmesan cheese

Zest of 1 lemon

3 eggs

2 ounces (55 g) fresh mozzarella cheese

¼ cup (32.5 g) peas, thawed if frozen

½ cup (63 g) all-purpose flour

1½ cups (75 g) panko bread crumbs

Kosher salt and pepper to taste

Vegetable oil for spraying

TOMATO SAUCE

2 tablespoons (30 ml) extra-virgin olive oil

4 cloves garlic, minced

¼ teaspoon red pepper flakes

1 can (28 ounces, or 800 g) crushed tomatoes

2 teaspoons granulated sugar

Kosher salt and pepper to taste

—
Makes 12 rice balls or 4 to 6 servings

Heat the stock in a small saucepan until simmering. Keep warm. In a Dutch oven, melt the butter over medium heat. Add the onion, season with salt, and sauté until softened, about 5 minutes. Add the rice and stir to coat with the butter. Cook the rice until slightly toasted, about 3 minutes. Add the wine and cook until the liquid has almost evaporated. Add 1 cup (240 ml) of the warm stock and stir to combine.

As the broth in the pan is absorbed by the rice, continue adding broth, a little bit at a time, stirring constantly. At first, the broth will be absorbed quickly, but as the rice becomes more saturated, it will absorb the broth more slowly and you will stir for longer before needing to add more. Keep the rice at a gentle simmer, adjusting the heat as

(continued)

(continued)

necessary. Continue adding broth, stirring and waiting until the broth is absorbed before adding more, until the rice is tender, creamy, and cooked all the way through, about 20 minutes.

When the rice is done, add the grated Parmesan, lemon zest, 1 of the eggs, and salt and pepper to taste and stir to combine. Spread the risotto out on a sheet pan, cover, and chill in the refrigerator for at least 1 hour and as long as overnight.

While the risotto cools, make the tomato sauce. Heat the olive oil in a medium saucepan over medium heat. Add the garlic and red pepper flakes and cook for a minute. Add the crushed tomatoes and sugar and bring to a boil. Reduce the heat and simmer until thickened, about 15 minutes. Season with salt and pepper. Keep warm.

Make the rice balls. Line a baking sheet with parchment paper. Form the risotto into twelve 2-inch (5 cm) balls. Flatten each ball into a disc and put a ½-inch (1.3 cm) piece of mozzarella and 5 to 6 peas in the center. Close the risotto around the filling and roll into a ball. Place the formed balls onto the baking sheet and chill until firm, at least 15 minutes.

Beat the remaining 2 eggs with 2 tablespoons (28 ml) of water. Place the flour on a small plate and spread the panko on a separate plate. Roll a rice ball in the flour, shaking off any excess, then coat with the egg mixture. Dredge the ball in the panko, pressing to make the crumbs adhere, and place the breaded rice ball on a lined baking sheet. Repeat with the remaining balls.

Spray the balls with oil and, working in batches, place 6 in a single layer in the air fryer basket. Cook at 400°F (200°C) for 10 to 12 minutes, flipping once halfway through, until browned and cooked through. Repeat with the remaining balls. Serve right away with warm tomato sauce.

Orange and Rosemary Roasted Chickpeas

Roasted chickpeas are vegan, gluten free, high in protein and fiber, and they happen to taste delicious. I think everyone can appreciate a snack that ticks all those boxes! Oven-roasting can take as long as 30 minutes, and the chickpeas do not always stay crisp once cool. Air frying chickpeas, however, ensures crispy results in half the time with only a drizzle of oil.

Enjoy these crisp roasted chickpeas out of hand or add them to salads and grain bowls such as the Sweet Potato and Farro Grain Bowls on page 78 for added protein and nutrition.

4 cups cooked chickpeas or
2 cans (15 ounces, or 425 g each)
chickpeas, rinsed and drained

2 tablespoons (30 ml) vegetable oil

1 teaspoon kosher salt

1 teaspoon cumin

1 teaspoon paprika

Zest of 1 orange

1 tablespoon (1.7 g) chopped
fresh rosemary

—
Makes 4 cups chickpeas

Make sure the chickpeas are completely dry prior to roasting. In a medium bowl, toss the chickpeas with oil, salt, cumin, and paprika. Preheat the air fryer to 400°F (200°C). Working in batches, spread the chickpeas in a single layer in the air fryer basket. Cook for 10 to 12 minutes until crisp, shaking once halfway through.

Return the warm chickpeas to the bowl and toss with the orange zest and rosemary. Allow to cool completly. They will continue to crisp as they cool. Store in an airtight container for up to 1 week.

Fried Pickles with Buttermilk-Herb Ranch Dressing

I vividly remember the first time I had fried pickles—a southern specialty dating back to the 1960s—on a trip to North Carolina. They were scalding hot right out of the fryer and served with a creamy ranch dipping sauce that cut through the brininess of the pickles. What a combination! Where had these been all my life?

Today, fried pickles are one of my favorite air fryer recipes. With a simple flour-egg-bread crumb coating and just a spritz of oil, these fried pickles come out extra crunchy and stay that way even after they cool down. I use pickle spears, not coins, because I find that they are easier to transfer in and out of the air fryer. Serve these fried pickles with a homemade buttermilk-herb ranch dressing and they may become one of your favorite recipes too.

BUTTERMILK-HERB RANCH DRESSING

¾ cup (175 g) mayonnaise

½ cup (115 g) sour cream

¼ cup (60 ml) buttermilk

¼ cup (25 g) chopped scallions

2 tablespoons (8 g) chopped fresh dill

1 tablespoon (3 g) chopped chives

½ teaspoon garlic powder

½ teaspoon onion powder

½ teaspoon cayenne pepper

Kosher salt and pepper to taste

FRIED PICKLES

1 jar (32 ounces, or 905 g) kosher dill pickles

¾ cup (94 g) all-purpose flour

Kosher salt and pepper to taste

2½ cups (125 g) panko bread crumbs

2 eggs beaten with 2 tablespoons (30 ml) water

Vegetable oil for spraying

—

Makes 32 to 36 spears or 6 to 8 servings

To make the dressing, in a medium bowl, whisk together the mayonnaise, sour cream, and buttermilk. Add the scallions, herbs, and seasonings and stir to combine. Cover the bowl and chill for at least 30 minutes prior to serving to allow the flavors to develop.

To make the fried pickles, cut each pickle into 4 spears and place the spears on paper towels to drain for at least 15 minutes. Place the flour on a plate and season with salt and pepper. Place the panko on a separate plate. Dip a pickle spear in the flour, shaking off any excess, then coat with egg mixture. Dredge the spear in the panko, pressing to make the crumbs adhere, and place the breaded spear on a lined baking sheet. Repeat with the remaining spears.

Spray the spears with oil and, working in batches, place them in a single layer in the air fryer basket. Cook at 400°F (200°C) for 8 to 10 minutes, flipping once halfway through. Serve with buttermilk ranch dressing.

Crispy Vegetable Spring Rolls

These crispy vegetable spring rolls are inspired by my daughter's favorite appetizer at our local pan-Asian noodle shop. But I argue that this version is even better. These rolls are long and skinny and have a shatteringly crispy exterior. To make sure your spring rolls come out super crispy, look for 8-inch (20 cm) square frozen spring roll sheets, not the thicker, doughier egg roll wrappers, which bubble when cooked.

It is important to allow the filling to cool completely before filling the spring rolls or else they may end up soggy. You can prepare the spring rolls up to several hours in advance and keep them covered in the refrigerator until needed. But they are best enjoyed fresh out of the air fryer! I like to serve mine with a bottled sweet chili sauce.

2 tablespoons (30 ml) vegetable oil plus more for brushing

5 ounces (140 g) shiitake mushrooms, diced

4 cups (360 g) sliced Napa cabbage

3 carrots, cut into thin matchsticks

1 bunch scallions, white and light green parts only, sliced

1 tablespoon (10 g) minced garlic

1 tablespoon (6 g) minced fresh ginger

2 tablespoons (30 ml) soy sauce

1 package (3.75 ounces, or 106 g) bean thread noodles (also called glass or cellophane noodles)

¼ teaspoon cornstarch

1 package (12 ounces, or 340 g) frozen spring roll wrappers, defrosted according to package instructions

—

Makes 14 spring rolls

In a large skillet, heat the oil over medium-high heat until shimmering. Add the mushrooms, cabbage, and carrots and sauté until softened, about 3 minutes. Add the scallions, garlic, and ginger and sauté an additional minute or two until fragrant. Add the soy sauce and, with a wooden spoon, scrape up any browned bits on the bottom of the pan. Remove from the heat and allow to cool completely before proceeding. If any liquid has accumulated in the bottom of the pan, pour it off so the filling is not soggy.

Place the bean thread noodles in a bowl and pour boiling water over them. Allow to stand for 10 minutes, until softened, and then drain. Remove 1 cup (150 g) of noodles and fold them into the vegetable mixture, reserving the remainder for another use.

Assemble the rolls. Dissolve the cornstarch in a small dish of warm water and place it nearby. Place 1 wrapper on a clean board with a corner pointing toward you. Keep the other wrappers covered with a damp towel to prevent them from drying out while you work. Place 3 tablespoons (26 g) of filling in a line above the bottom corner, leaving space on both sides. Pick up the bottom corner and begin rolling the wrapper tightly around the filling until you reach the middle. Tightly fold in the sides and continue rolling until you reach the top corner. Dab a small bit of the water-cornstarch mixture on the top corner and seal the roll closed. Place the completed roll on a lined baking sheet and cover with a towel while you complete the remaining rolls. (Spring rolls may be frozen at this point.)

To cook, brush the outside of each roll lightly with oil. Working in batches of 5 at a time, place the rolls in the air fryer and cook at 400°F (200°C) for 8 to 10 minutes, flipping once halfway through. (To cook frozen rolls add 5 to 6 minutes to the cooking time.) Serve immediately with a dipping sauce.

Chinese Takeout Egg Rolls with Soy-Vinegar Dipping Sauce

These air-fried egg rolls make a fun hors d'oeuvres for a party and can even be prepared in advance and frozen. Look for the thick egg roll wrappers that are typically 7-inch (18 cm) squares, as opposed to the thinner, larger spring roll wrappers. You want these wrappers to bubble as they cook, just like restaurant egg rolls. Pork filling is traditional, but ground chicken will also work well for a lighter version.

EGG ROLLS

3 tablespoons (45 ml) soy sauce, divided

1 tablespoon (15 ml) mirin or rice wine

1 pound (455 g) ground pork or dark meat chicken

3 tablespoons (45 ml) vegetable oil plus more for brushing

4 cups (280 g) shredded Napa cabbage

5 ounces (140 g) shiitake mushrooms, minced

¼ cup (25 g) sliced scallions

1 teaspoon grated fresh ginger

1 clove garlic, minced

¼ teaspoon cornstarch

1 package (16 ounces, or 455 g) refrigerated or frozen egg roll wrappers, thawed if frozen

SOY-VINEGAR DIPPING SAUCE

¼ cup (60 ml) soy sauce

¼ cup (60 ml) rice vinegar

1 scallion, white and light green parts only, sliced

1 teaspoon granulated sugar

Pinch red pepper flakes

Pinch sesame seeds

—

Makes 25 egg rolls

To make the egg rolls, combine 1 tablespoon (15 ml) of the soy sauce, the mirin, and the ground meat in a bowl and stir to combine. Cover and refrigerate for 10 to 15 minutes.

In a large skillet, heat the oil over medium-high heat until shimmering. Add the cabbage, mushrooms, and scallions and cook, stirring constantly, until wilted. Add the marinated meat, the remaining 2 tablespoons (30 ml) of soy sauce, ginger, and garlic, and cook until the meat is no longer pink, about 3 minutes. Remove from the heat and allow the filling to cool completely. If any liquid has accumulated in the bottom of the pan, pour it off so the filling is not soggy.

Assemble the rolls. Dissolve the cornstarch in a small dish of warm water and place it nearby. Place 1 wrapper on a clean board with a corner pointing toward you. Keep the other wrappers covered with a damp towel to prevent them from drying out while you work. Place 2 tablespoons (25 g) of filling in a line above the bottom corner, leaving space on both sides. Pick up the bottom corner and begin rolling the wrapper tightly around the filling until you reach the middle. Tightly fold in the sides and continue rolling until you reach the top corner. Dab a small bit of the water-cornstarch mixture on the top corner and seal the roll closed. Place the completed roll on a lined baking sheet and cover with a towel while you complete the remaining rolls.

To make the soy-vinegar dipping sauce, combine the soy sauce, rice vinegar, scallion, sugar, red pepper flakes, and sesame seeds in a small bowl. Whisk until the sugar is dissolved.

To cook, brush the outside of each roll lightly with oil. Working in batches of 5 at a time, place the rolls in the air fryer and cook at 400°F (200°C) for 8 to 10 minutes, flipping once halfway through. Serve immediately with soy-vinegar dipping sauce.

To cook frozen egg rolls, cook at 400°F (200°C) until browned all over but not burnt, approximately 15 to 20 minutes, flipping once halfway through.

Pork and Cabbage Gyoza

Every cuisine has its dumpling, and making them is usually a labor of love. This recipe for Japanese-inspired *gyoza*, a pork and cabbage dumpling with a characteristic pleated shape, is no exception. Enlist friends and family members to help fill and fold the dumplings and the work will go that much quicker. The oil and water mixture serves to fry and steam the gyoza at the same time so that they cook up deliciously crispy on top and soft on the sides.

This recipe makes approximately 4 dozen gyoza, which is perfect for a large party. If you don't need that many, freeze any extra dumplings right after making them. These frozen gyoza can be cooked in small batches whenever the mood strikes.

1 small head Napa cabbage (about 1 pound [455 g])

2 teaspoons kosher salt

1 pound (455 g) ground pork

½ cup (50 g) minced scallions

1 tablespoon (10 g) minced garlic

1 teaspoon minced fresh ginger

1 teaspoon minced fresh chives

1 teaspoon granulated sugar

1 teaspoon soy sauce

48 to 50 wonton or dumpling wrappers, thawed if frozen

1 tablespoon (15 ml) vegetable oil

Soy-Vinegar Dipping Sauce (page 46)

—
Makes 48 dumplings

Remove the cabbage core and slice the leaves thinly. Finely mince the slices. Place the minced cabbage in a colander set over a large bowl and sprinkle with the salt. Let the cabbage rest for at least 15 minutes while the salt draws out the excess moisture. Wrap the cabbage in a clean kitchen towel or cheesecloth and squeeze out as much liquid as possible. Place the drained cabbage in a large bowl. Combine the cabbage with the pork, scallions, garlic, ginger, chives, sugar, and soy sauce and knead with your hands to combine.

To fill the dumplings, set up a work station with a wooden cutting board, a bowl with the filling, a small bowl of water, the stack of dumpling wrappers (wrapped in plastic to prevent them from drying out), and a lined baking sheet. Place 1 wrapper on the cutting board. Spoon 2 teaspoons filling in the center. Moisten the edges of the wrapper with water. Pinch the sides of the wrapper together, pleating 1 side of the dumpling in the traditional manner, if desired. Place the filled dumpling on the baking sheet and cover with a clean towel. Repeat until you have used all the wrappers and filling. (Dumplings may be frozen at this point. Freeze on the sheet until firm, then pack into a gallon-size freezer bag for storage.)

To cook the dumplings, preheat the air fryer to 360°F (182°C). Combine the vegetable oil with ½ cup (120 ml) water in a small bowl. Brush the outside of 6 dumplings with the oil-water mixture and place in the air fryer basket. Sprinkle additional oil-water mixture on the basket. Cook the dumplings for 8 to 10 minutes, flipping once halfway through. Leave the dumplings in the air fryer with the power off for 2 minutes. Remove and cook as many additional dumplings as needed in the same manner. (Dumplings may be cooked from frozen in the same manner.)

Serve warm with Soy-Vinegar Dipping Sauce (page 46).

Crab Rangoon

A staple of Chinese and Thai restaurant menus—although it was surely invented in America—crab rangoon is a perennial favorite. Like egg rolls and gyoza, crab rangoons come out golden and crispy in the air fryer without all the mess and oil of deep-frying. Serve these air fried crab rangoons at your next cocktail party and watch them disappear.

Any number of dipping sauces work well with crab rangoon, from Soy-Vinegar Dipping Sauce (page 46) to a bottled sweet chili sauce to a spicy Chinese mustard. Better yet, offer all three and let your guests decide.

5 ounces (140 g) lump crabmeat, drained and patted with paper towels to remove excess liquid

4 ounces (115 g) cream cheese, at room temperature

2 scallions, white and green parts only, sliced, plus more for garnish

1½ teaspoons toasted sesame oil

1 teaspoon Worcestershire sauce

Kosher salt and pepper

24 wonton wrappers (2 inch [5 cm]), thawed if frozen

3 tablespoons (45 ml) vegetable oil, for brushing

—
Makes 24 pieces, to serve 6 to 8

Combine the lump crabmeat, cream cheese, scallions, sesame oil, Worcestershire sauce, and salt and pepper to taste in a medium bowl. Stir until the mixture is completely smooth.

To assemble, take a wonton wrapper and place 1 scant teaspoon of filling in the center of the wrapper. (Do not overfill.) With a finger dipped in water, moisten the edges of 2 adjacent sides of the wrapper. Fold in half to form a triangle. Place the filled triangle on a plate or baking sheet lined with parchment paper. Repeat with the remaining filling until all the wonton wrappers have been filled. (Uncooked rangoons can be wrapped and kept frozen for 1 to 2 weeks. Do not thaw before cooking.)

Preheat the air fryer to 350°F (180°C). To cook, brush the rangoons lightly with oil on both sides and arrange in batches in the air fryer basket, 6 to 8 at a time. Cook the rangoons until crisp and golden, about 10 minutes. Garnish the cooked crab rangoons with sliced scallions and serve immediately with your favorite dipping sauce.

Roasted Garlic Guacamole with Homemade Tortilla Chips

I used to make homemade tortilla chips by frying one tortilla at a time in oil on the stove. It was both messy and time-consuming. How liberating, then, to be able to make homemade tortilla chips anytime I want in the air fryer with much less oil and bother! Serve these homemade chips with soups, dips, or use them to make epic nachos. Store-bought chips pale in comparison.

Roasting garlic in the air fryer is another revelation. It takes half the time of the oven. Here roasted garlic brings a mellow sweetness to creamy guacamole with just a hint of heat from a roasted jalapeño pepper.

ROASTED GARLIC GUACAMOLE

1 head garlic

1 teaspoon vegetable oil

1 jalapeño pepper

4 ripe avocados

3 tablespoons (45 ml) freshly squeezed lime juice

1 teaspoon cumin

1 teaspoon kosher salt

Pinch cayenne pepper

½ red onion, diced

2 plum tomatoes, seeded and diced

TORTILLA CHIPS

12 corn tortillas

Vegetable oil for brushing

3 teaspoons kosher salt

—

Serves 4 to 6

To make the roasted garlic, cut off the top third of the head of garlic, exposing the tops of the cloves, and drizzle with oil. Wrap in foil and place garlic in the basket of the air fryer. Cook at 400°F (200°C) for 20 to 25 minutes until the cloves are soft. Remove the garlic from the air fryer, unwrap, and allow to cool. Squeeze the garlic cloves into a large bowl.

Place the jalapeño pepper in the basket of the air fryer and cook at 400°F (200°C) until the skin is blackened on all sides, turning 2 or 3 times, approximately 12 minutes. Remove the pepper and cover for 10 minutes. When the pepper is cool enough to handle, remove the charred outer skin. Remove the seeds and dice the pepper. Add to the bowl with the roasted garlic.

Halve the avocados and remove the pits. Scoop the avocado into the bowl with the roasted garlic and pepper. Mash together. Add the lime juice, cumin, 1 teaspoon of the salt, and cayenne pepper and stir to combine. Stir in the onion and tomatoes. Taste and adjust the seasoning. Cover the guacamole with plastic wrap and refrigerate until needed.

To make the tortilla chips, brush the corn tortillas with oil and sprinkle each one with ¼ teaspoon salt. Cut each tortilla into 6 wedges. Preheat the air fryer to 400°F (200°C). Working in batches, spread the tortilla chips in a single layer in the basket of the air fryer. Cook for 4 to 6 minutes, turning once halfway through, until crisp. Remove and repeat with the remaining chips. Allow the chips to cool before serving.

Smoky Eggplant Dip with Homemade Pita Chips

Baba ghanoush, a smoky spread made with roasted eggplant, is a classic Middle Eastern mezze and the inspiration for this dip. Many people find eggplant to be tricky to cook because it is watery and absorbs oil like a sponge. Cooking eggplant in the air fryer, however, is nearly foolproof and uses much less oil than other methods. The heat of the air fryer caramelizes the eggplant and removes excess moisture, leading to a smooth, richly flavored spread.

Pita chips are an increasingly popular accompaniment to all kinds of spreads and dips, but the store-bought kind are expensive. You can save money and cut down on the fat by making your own crispy pita chips in the air fryer using regular pita bread brushed with a little olive oil.

3 medium eggplants, cubed

6 tablespoons (90 ml) vegetable oil

Kosher salt and pepper to taste

2 tablespoons (30 ml) extra-virgin olive oil plus extra for brushing

2 tablespoons (30 g) tahini

Juice of 2 lemons

3 cloves garlic

1 teaspoon cumin

½ teaspoon smoked paprika

5 pita rounds

—

Serves 4 to 6

Drizzle the eggplant with the vegetable oil and toss to combine. Season with salt and pepper. Working in batches, spread the eggplant in a single layer in the basket of the air fryer. Cook at 400°F (200°C) for 15 minutes, turning the pieces halfway through.

Place the cooked eggplant in the bowl of a food processor. Add the olive oil, tahini, lemon juice, garlic, cumin, and smoked paprika and process until smooth. Add salt and pepper to taste. Transfer the eggplant dip to a bowl, cover, and chill until needed. (If possible, make the eggplant dip ahead of time and chill it for several hours or overnight to allow the flavors to develop.)

To make the pita chips, brush each side of the pita rounds with olive oil and cut into 6 wedges. Working in batches, place the wedges of pita in a single layer in the basket of the air fryer. Cook at 375°F (190°C) for 6 to 8 minutes, turning once halfway through, until the chips are browned on both sides and crisp.

Just prior to serving, drizzle the eggplant dip with extra virgin olive oil, preferably a fruity finishing oil, and serve with pita chips.

Tandoori Yogurt Dip with Naan Breadsticks

Just like its cousin, pita, the South Asian flatbread naan, when brushed with oil and air-fried, makes a crispy, sturdy chip that won't break even when you scoop up the chunkiest dip. Today, most grocery stores carry packaged naan in the bakery section, making it easy to enjoy this Indian restaurant favorite at home.

Keeping with the South Asian theme, I pair these naan chips with a cool and creamy yogurt dip flavored with warm tandoori spices.

2 cups (460 g) plain Greek yogurt, preferably full fat

1 clove garlic, minced

1 tablespoon (6 g) Tandoori Spice Mix (see below), divided

Juice and zest of ½ lemon

1 tablespoon (15 ml) extra-virgin olive oil plus extra for brushing

3 large naan

TANDOORI SPICE MIX

1 teaspoon cumin

1 teaspoon coriander

1 teaspoon ginger

1 teaspoon kosher salt

½ teaspoon paprika

½ teaspoon cayenne pepper

½ teaspoon turmeric

—

Serves 4 to 6

To make the tandoori spice mix, whisk together the spices in a small bowl until well combined.

In a large bowl, combine the yogurt, garlic, 1 tablespoon (6 g) of the tandoori spice mix, lemon juice and zest, and olive oil. Stir until thoroughly mixed. Refrigerate for 1 hour to allow the flavors to develop.

To make the naan chips, brush the naan with olive oil and sprinkle each piece with some of the tandoori spice mix to taste. Slice the bread into 1½-inch (4 cm) strips and cut the longer strips in half. Working in batches, arrange the naan chips in a single layer in the basket of the air fryer. Cook at 360°F (182°C) for 4 to 6 minutes, turning once halfway through, until browned on both sides and crispy. Serve the naan chips warm with the yogurt dip.

Fried Green Tomatoes with Rémoulade

Gardeners and farmers market devotees are often confronted with piles of green tomatoes at the end of summer. Recently, I have noticed them in grocery stores year-round. What better way to use up these firm, tart unripe tomatoes than to batter them and fry them?

The air fryer makes it easy to enjoy fried green tomatoes any time of year without heating up a pot of oil or, as is traditional, bacon grease. These are best enjoyed hot, right out of the air fryer, with a tangy dipping sauce, such as this Louisiana-style rémoulade. Fried green tomatoes work on their own as a side dish for grilled steak or chicken, but you can also add them to a salad or even put them in a sandwich. Try a fried green tomato slider or a fried green tomato BLT.

RÉMOULADE

1 cup (225 g) mayonnaise

3 tablespoons (45 g) mustard

1 tablespoon (15 ml) freshly squeezed lemon juice

1 tablespoon (8.6 g) capers

1 tablespoon (1.3 g) chopped fresh flat-leaf parsley

2 scallions, white and light green part only, sliced

2 teaspoons Louisiana-style hot sauce

1½ teaspoons Cajun seasoning

½ teaspoon garlic powder

½ teaspoon black pepper

FRIED GREEN TOMATOES

3 green tomatoes

¾ cup (94 g) all-purpose flour

¾ cup (105 g) cornmeal, preferably finely ground

1½ teaspoons kosher salt

1 teaspoon black pepper

½ teaspoon cayenne pepper

2 eggs

¼ cup (60 ml) buttermilk (regular milk is an acceptable substitute)

Vegetable oil for spraying

—

Serves 4

Combine all the rémoulade ingredients in a medium-size bowl. Cover and chill for at least 1 hour to allow the flavors to develop.

To make the fried green tomatoes, trim the ends off each tomato and slice into ¼-inch-thick (6 mm) slices. Place the slices on a paper towel–lined plate to absorb excess liquid.

Place the flour, cornmeal, salt, black pepper, and cayenne pepper on a second plate, stirring with a fork to combine. Whisk the eggs and buttermilk together in a shallow bowl.

Dip a third of the tomato slices in the egg mixture then dredge them in the flour-cornmeal mixture, shaking off any excess. (Do not coat the tomato slices until right before you cook them.) Spray both sides with oil, making sure to coat the slices well. Place the slices in the basket of the air fryer and cook at 400°F (200°C) for 10 minutes, flipping the slices once halfway through. (If you see spots that look like dry flour, spray those with additional oil.) While the first batch of tomatoes is cooking, batter the next batch. Repeat the process with the remaining slices.

Serve the fried green tomatoes hot out of the fryer with rémoulade sauce.

Low Country Hush Puppies

Whether you are at a fish fry or a southern barbecue joint, chances are, hush puppies are on the menu. These deep-fried balls of cornmeal batter are sometimes known as corn dodgers when north of the Mason-Dixon line. They are almost always served as an accompaniment to fried catfish.

In this classic recipe, the acid from the buttermilk reacts with the baking soda to leaven these hush puppies. The buttermilk also adds tanginess that is a nice contrast with the sweet corn batter. A little bit of melted butter in the batter adds richness, and a quick spray of oil makes the outside brown and crispy. To make these hush puppies spicy, simply add a pinch of cayenne pepper or a dash of hot sauce to the batter.

1 cup (140 g) cornmeal, preferably finely ground

½ cup (63 g) all-purpose flour

1 tablespoon (13 g) granulated sugar

1 teaspoon kosher salt

½ teaspoon baking soda

½ teaspoon black pepper

1 cup (240 ml) buttermilk

2 tablespoons (28 g) unsalted butter, melted

Vegetable oil for spraying

—
Makes 12 hush puppies, to serve 4

Whisk together the cornmeal, flour, sugar, salt, baking soda, and pepper in a medium bowl. Make a well in the center of the dry ingredients. Pour in the buttermilk and melted butter and stir with a fork until the batter just comes together. Let the batter rest for 10 minutes.

Preheat the air fryer to 390°F (199°C). Using a small cookie scoop or spoon, scoop 5 or 6 circles of batter approximately 1½ inches (4 cm) in diameter directly onto the basket of the air fryer. Spray with oil. Cook until the outside is firm and browned and the inside is cooked through, approximately 10 minutes. Remove from the air fryer. Repeat with the remaining batter. Serve warm with butter.

Elotes (Mexican Street Corn)

Does your local taqueria serve *elotes*, or have you ever been at a street festival and spied this grilled Mexican corn slathered with a creamy sauce and topped with crumbled cheese? I think elotes is one of the very best ways to serve corn-on-the-cob, and I cannot believe how quick and easy it is to make in the air fryer. Serve these air fryer elotes alongside your favorite Mexican-inspired meals and Taco Tuesday will never be the same!

Crema is a smooth, velvety Mexican condiment that is made by culturing heavy cream with buttermilk and seasoning it with lime and salt. It is similar to sour cream in tanginess but thinner in consistency. It is readily available in the dairy section of most stores, but, in a pinch, you can use sour cream that you have thinned with a little cream or buttermilk. You can also make crema at home, but it will take several hours to set up at room temperature.

¼ cup (60 ml) Mexican crema

¼ cup (60 g) mayonnaise

1 lime

½ teaspoon garlic powder

Pinch cayenne pepper plus more for garnish

4 shucked ears corn

2 tablespoons (28 g) unsalted butter, melted

¼ cup (38 g) crumbled queso fresco (Mexican fresh cheese)

¼ cup (4 g) chopped cilantro

—
Serves 4 as a side dish

Whisk together the crema, mayonnaise, the zest from the lime, the garlic powder, and a pinch of the cayenne pepper in a small bowl. Set aside.

Preheat the air fryer to 400°F (200°C). Brush the ears of corn with the melted butter. Place the corn in the air fryer and cook, rotating 2 or 3 times, until browned on all sides, 10 to 12 minutes. Remove the ears of corn to a serving platter.

Brush the ears with the crema and mayonnaise mixture. Sprinkle the crumbled queso fresco and chopped cilantro on top of the corn. Spritz the corn with the juice from the lime and sprinkle with additional cayenne pepper, if desired. Serve immediately.

Prosciutto-Wrapped Asparagus

This easy-yet-elegant dish is a worthy use of local spring and early summer asparagus. When selecting asparagus for this recipe, choose thicker ones because they have more flavor and the thin ones tend to scorch. The prosciutto becomes wonderfully crispy in the dry heat of the air fryer while the asparagus stays crisp-tender.

You can serve this prosciutto-wrapped asparagus as a first course for a dinner party or as a quick-cooking side dish. Your family will be sure to eat their vegetables when they are wrapped in prosciutto!

12 asparagus spears, tough stems removed

6 thin slices prosciutto, each piece cut in half

1 tablespoon (15 ml) olive oil

½ teaspoon kosher salt

½ teaspoon black pepper

—

Makes 12 asparagus spears or 4 servings

Carefully wrap 1 prosciutto piece around each asparagus spear. Drizzle with olive oil and sprinkle with salt and pepper. Arrange the asparagus spears in a single layer in the air fryer basket.

Cook at 350°F (180°C) for 8 to 10 minutes or until the prosciutto is crispy and the asparagus is tender. Serve immediately.

Caribbean Yuca Fries

Yuca, also known as cassava, is a starchy tuber common in Latin and Caribbean cooking. Like potatoes, yuca makes outstanding fries with a crispy exterior and an exceptionally fluffy and starchy interior. When I began cooking with an air fryer, I wondered if it would produce yuca fries as good as the ones at my local Cuban restaurant. The answer is, it does, but there's just one catch: you have to boil the yuca before you can fry it.

Okay, there's actually another catch. This skinny tuber has a rough brown exterior like tree bark that must be removed before cooking. This is not hard, but if you are intimidated by the odd-looking knobby root, look for peeled frozen yuca pieces instead. Serve these yuca fries alongside Jalea (Peruvian Fried Seafood with Salsa Criolla, page 120).

3 yuca roots
Vegetable oil for spraying
1 teaspoon kosher salt

—

Serves 4 as a side dish

Trim the ends off the yuca roots and cut each one into 2 or 3 pieces depending on the length. Have a bowl of water ready. Peel off the rough outer skin with a paring knife or sharp vegetable peeler. Halve each piece of yuca lengthwise. Place the peeled pieces in a bowl of water to prevent them from oxidizing and turning brown.

Fill a large pot with water and bring to a boil over high heat. Season well with salt. Add the yuca pieces to the water and cook until they are tender enough to be pierced with a fork, but not falling apart, approximately 12 to 15 minutes. Drain. Some of the yuca pieces will have fibrous string running down the center. Remove it. Cut the yuca into 2 or 3 pieces to resemble thick-cut french fries.

Working in batches, arrange the yuca fries in a single layer in the air fryer basket. Spray with oil. Cook at 400°F (200°C) for 10 minutes, turning the fries halfway through, until the outside of the fries is crisp and browned and the inside fluffy. Repeat with the remaining fries. Spray the cooked yuca with oil and toss with 1 teaspoon salt.

Tempura Shishito Peppers

Shishito peppers have migrated from restaurant menus to farmers markets and now to grocery stores and our kitchen tables. These small, wrinkly Japanese green peppers are mild and sweet—except when they're not. You see, one in ten of these otherwise sweet peppers is actually quite spicy. Just one of the fun pranks Mother Nature plays on us, like snowstorms in April.

Shishito peppers are very easy to cook at home, especially with the air fryer. You can simply toss the peppers with oil and blister them in the air fryer for 7 to 8 minutes. But I actually like to coat the peppers in a light, tempura-like batter before cooking to give them a thin, crispy exterior. Serve these lightly battered peppers with Soy-Vinegar Dipping Sauce (page 46).

1 cup (125 g) all-purpose flour

½ cup (64 g) cornstarch

2 teaspoons baking soda

1 teaspoon kosher salt

1 cup (240 ml) seltzer water or club soda

8 ounces (225 g) shishito peppers

Vegetable oil for spraying

—

Serves 4 as a side dish

To make the tempura batter, whisk together the flour, cornstarch, baking soda, and salt in a large bowl. Slowly whisk in the seltzer water until you have created a thick batter. Place a cooling rack over a board lined with wax or parchment paper. Using the stem as handle, dip a shishito pepper in the batter then tap it against the side of the bowl several times to remove any excess. Place the battered peppers on the rack. Repeat with half the peppers, waiting to batter the other half.

Brush the basket of the air fryer lightly with oil to prevent sticking. Arrange the battered peppers in a single layer in the air fryer basket. Spray the peppers with oil. Cook at 350°F (180°C) or 7 to 8 minutes until the peppers are browned on the outside and tender on the inside. (Do not be alarmed if you hear the peppers popping in the air fryer. This is normal.) While the first batch of peppers is cooking, batter the remaining peppers.

Remove the first batch of peppers from the air fryer and place on a serving plate or platter. Cook the second batch of peppers in the same manner as the first. Serve the peppers warm with Soy-Vinegar Dipping Sauce (page 46).

Spicy Maple-Soy Brussels Sprouts

When did Brussels sprouts go from everyone's most-hated to most-loved vegetable? Probably around when we figured out that roasting these littlest members of the Brassica family caramelizes and crisps up the outside while making the inside fork-tender. The latest development in Brussels sprouts' rise to the top of the vegetable pyramid? The air fryer. Its high heat and fast air turns out fantastic roasted Brussels sprouts in less than twenty minutes.

This salty-sweet maple-soy glaze was inspired by the spicy fried Brussels sprouts appetizer at one of my children's favorite restaurants in Naples, Florida, where we spend the holidays. The sriracha brings the heat here, so if you prefer less spicy Brussels, simply reduce the amount.

½ pounds (680 g) Brussels sprouts, trimmed and, if large, halved

1 tablespoon (15 ml) extra-virgin olive oil

½ teaspoon kosher salt

3 tablespoons (45 ml) soy sauce

2 tablespoons (40 g) maple syrup

Juice and zest of 1 lime

1 clove garlic, minced

1 tablespoon (15 ml) sriracha

—
Serves 4 as a side dish

Toss the Brussels sprouts with the olive oil and salt. Working in batches if necessary, arrange the sprouts in a single layer in the basket of the air fryer. Cook at 375°F (190°C) until browned, crispy, and fork-tender, 15 to 20 minutes.

While the Brussels sprouts are cooking, combine the soy sauce, maple syrup, lime zest and juice, garlic, and sriracha in a small saucepan. Bring to a boil over medium heat. Reduce the heat and simmer until thickened and slightly syrupy, 5 to 7 minutes.

Remove the Brussels sprouts from the air fryer. (If you were not able to fit all the Brussels sprouts in the air fryer, cook the remaining Brussels sprouts in the same manner.) Place the Brussels sprouts in a serving bowl and drizzle the maple-soy sauce over them. Stir to coat the sprouts with the sauce and serve warm.

Sweet and Smoky Candied Pecans

These candied pecans are a wonderful nibble to serve with drinks, but they also make a delightful addition to salads, such as the Tropical Glazed Chicken Salad on page 84.

Nuts can go from toasty to burnt in the air fryer in less than a minute, and it would be a shame to burn such an expensive ingredient. Keep a close watch on your pecans and check them every minute or so after the first 5 minutes. They will still seem soft and sticky when they are done, but they crisp up as they cool. Judge whether the nuts are sufficiently toasted by smell and taste, not by looks.

1 pound (455 g) pecan halves

2 egg whites

½ cup (115 g) brown sugar

1 tablespoon (7 g) cumin

2 teaspoons smoked paprika

2 teaspoons kosher salt

—
**Makes approximately
4 cups pecans**

Toss the pecans with the egg whites in a medium bowl. Add the sugar and spices and toss to coat the pecans with the seasoning.

Place half the pecans in the basket of the air fryer. Cook at 300°F (150°C) for 10 to 12 minutes, checking frequently and shaking the basket, until the nuts taste toasty and caramelized but not burnt. Remove the basket from the air fryer and spread the pecans on a baking sheet to cool. (They will firm up and become crispy as they cool.) Repeat with the remaining pecans. Store in an airtight container until needed. Will last up to 2 weeks.

Avocado Fries with Pomegranate Molasses

It would have never occurred to me to bread and fry slices of avocado before I purchased my air fryer, but now this is my new favorite way to eat avocado. These avocado fries are so simple that older kids and teens can make them by themselves for a healthy yet irresistibly tasty snack.

For best results, look for ripe but still firm avocados that won't fall apart when sliced. I find that even firm avocados will break if you try to dip them like a french fry, so I prefer to drizzle these avocado fries with a thin sauce. My favorite is tart, intense pomegranate molasses, which is nothing more than pomegranate juice that has been reduced and thickened to a syrup. Look for it with other Middle Eastern ingredients at your grocery store. If you don't have pomegranate molasses, a good balsamic vinegar works as well.

1 cup (50 g) panko bread crumbs

1 teaspoon kosher salt plus more for sprinkling

1 teaspoon garlic powder

½ teaspoon cayenne pepper

2 ripe but firm avocados

1 egg beaten with 1 tablespoon (15 ml) water

Vegetable oil for spraying

Pomegranate molasses for serving (optional)

—
Makes 16 fries, to serve 4

Whisk together the panko, salt, and spices on a plate. Cut each avocado in half and remove the pit. Cut each avocado half into 4 slices and scoop the slices out with a large spoon, taking care to keep the slices intact.

Dip each avocado slice in the egg wash and then dredge it in the panko. Place the breaded avocado slices on a plate. Working in 2 batches, arrange half of the avocado slices in a single layer in the basket of the air fryer. Spray lightly with oil. Cook the slices for 7 to 8 minutes at 375°F (190°C), turning once halfway through. Remove the cooked slices to a platter and repeat with the remaining avocado slices.

Sprinkle the warm avocado slices with salt and drizzle with pomegranate molasses, if using.

KFC (Korean Fried Cauliflower)

Korean fried *chicken* has become justifiably famous in the past decade for its extra-crispy exterior and the spicy and sweet glaze—made with the Korean chile paste *gochujang*—that coats every morsel. It didn't take long for vegetable lovers to replace the chicken with another ingredient that starts with c: cauliflower.

You will notice that, in this recipe, the cauliflower is coated in a wet batter, not the usual flour-egg-panko breading. The batter, although wet, is sticky enough that the air fryer fan will not blow it off and, once cooked, it creates a light, crispy coating that grips the spicy sauce.

KOREAN BBQ SAUCE

3 tablespoons (45 ml) soy sauce

2 tablespoons (38 g) gochujang

2 tablespoons (30 ml) rice vinegar

2 tablespoons (30 g) brown sugar

2 cloves garlic, minced

1 tablespoon (6 g) fresh ginger, minced

1 tablespoon (15 ml) sesame or vegetable oil

½ cup (120 ml) warm water

FRIED CAULIFLOWER

1 cup (125 g) all-purpose flour

½ cup (65 g) cornstarch

2 teaspoons baking soda

1 teaspoon kosher salt

1 cup (240 ml) water

1 head cauliflower, cut into florets

Vegetable oil for spraying

1 teaspoon sesame seeds

2 scallions, white and light green parts only, sliced

—

Serves 4

To make the sauce, whisk together the soy sauce, gochujang, vinegar, brown sugar, garlic, and ginger in a large bowl. While whisking, slowly pour in the oil in a steady stream and continue whisking until emulsified. Gradually whisk in the warm water until you reach a thin sauce-like consistency; you may not need the entire ½ cup of water depending on how thick your gochujang is. Set aside.

To make the batter for the cauliflower, whisk together the flour, cornstarch, baking soda, and salt in a large bowl. Slowly whisk in the water until you have created a thick batter. Place a cooling rack over a board lined with wax or parchment paper. Dip the cauliflower florets in the batter and then place them on the rack to allow the excess batter to drip off.

Spray the basket of the air fryer lightly with oil. Working in batches, arrange the battered florets in a single layer in the air fryer basket. Cook at 350°F (180°C) for 12 minutes until the florets are browned on the outside and tender on the inside.

Place the cooked florets in the bowl with the sauce and toss to coat. Garnish with sesame seeds and scallions. Repeat with the remaining florets. Serve warm.

Roasted Red Pepper and Feta Salad

This eye-catching side dish begs to be made during summer when sweet bell peppers and fresh basil are at their peak. This recipe serves four generously as a side dish, but you could easily double or even triple the recipe if feeding a crowd. Because this dish works well at room temperature and can sit for long periods with no ill effects, it is ideal for bringing to a cookout or potluck.

The ease of roasting red peppers in the air fryer is a revelation. No need to stand over a hot skillet or turn on the big oven and heat up the whole house. I also use the air fryer to toast the pine nuts in this recipe. Toasting brings out the flavor of pine nuts, but they can go from toasted to burnt rather quickly, so keep a close eye on them.

4 bell peppers, red, orange, or yellow or a combination thereof

1 tablespoon (15 ml) extra-virgin olive oil plus extra for drizzling

2 tablespoons (18 g) pine nuts

2 ounces (55 g) Greek feta cheese in brine, crumbled

1 teaspoon red wine vinegar

1 sprig basil, leaves removed and cut into ribbons

—
Serves 4 as a side dish

If your air fryer has a deep basket, roast the peppers whole. Simply brush the outside of the peppers with the olive oil and place them in the air fryer basket. You will likely be able to fit 2 or 3 peppers at the most. Roast at 400°F (200°C), turning several times, until blackened on all sides, 25 to 30 minutes.

If you have a toaster oven–style air fryer, you will likely not be able fit a whole pepper in the basket. Instead, cut peppers into 3 or 4 pieces, removing the core and seeds. Brush the outside of the peppers with the olive oil and arrange the pieces skin side up in a single layer in the basket. Roast at 400°F (200°C) until the skin is charred, about 15 minutes.

Place the cooked peppers in a bowl and cover with a clean towel. Allow the peppers to steam for 10 minutes. While the peppers are steaming, toast the pine nuts. Place the pine nuts in the pizza pan insert for the air fryer. Place the pan in the air fryer basket. Toast at 325°F (170°C) until the pine nuts are lightly browned and smell toasty, 4 to 5 minutes. Check frequently to make sure the pine nuts do not scorch. Remove from the pan and set aside.

Once the peppers are cool enough to handle, remove the skin from the peppers and, if necessary, the seeds and core. Tear whole peppers into 3 or 4 pieces.

Arrange the peppers on a serving platter. Top with crumbled feta and toasted pine nuts. Drizzle the peppers with additional olive oil and vinegar. Scatter basil over the peppers. Serve warm or at room temperature.

CHAPTER 3
Vegetarian Main Courses

Falafel with Israeli Salad   70

Zucchini Rice Fritters   71

Zucchini, Spinach, and Feta Pancakes
with Tzatziki   72

Cauliflower Steaks with Tahini Sauce   74

Kale and Mushroom Empanadas   75

Loaded Baked Potatoes with Broccoli and
Cheddar Cheese Sauce   76

Sweet Potato and Farro Grain Bowls with
Creamy Herb Dressing   78

Eggplant Parmesan   80

Paneer Tikka   81

Falafel with Israeli Salad

It is surprisingly easy to make crispy, herbaceous falafel at home, especially if you can cook them in an air fryer as opposed to deep-frying. For best results, however, you must start with softened, but not cooked, dried chickpeas. Canned chickpeas are too soft to form the coarse-ground texture needed for falafel. To soften dry chickpeas, you can soak them overnight or—if planning ahead is not your strong suit—you can boil them quickly and then soak them for just an hour.

It would be most traditional to serve these falafel with Tahini Sauce (page 74), but if you do not care for tahini, or if, like me, someone in your family is allergic to sesame, Tzatziki (page 72) would make a delicious accompaniment.

FALAFEL

8 ounces (225 g) dried chickpeas

1 cup (60 g) fresh flat-leaf or Italian parsley, lightly packed

3 cloves garlic

3 scallions, white and light green parts only

1 teaspoon kosher salt

1 teaspoon cumin

½ teaspoon coriander

Pinch cayenne pepper

Juice of ½ lemon

Vegetable oil for spraying

ISRAELI SALAD

2 red bell peppers, cored and chopped

1 English or hothouse cucumber, thickly sliced and quartered

1 small red onion, diced

3 tablespoons (45 ml) extra-virgin olive oil

2 tablespoons (30 ml) red wine vinegar

1 teaspoon kosher salt

Freshly ground black pepper

—

Makes 12 falafels, to serve 4

To make the falafel, soak the dried chickpeas in 10 cups (2.4 L) of water overnight and drain. Alternatively, combine the chickpeas and 10 cups (2.4 L) of water in a large saucepan. Bring to a boil over high heat and boil for 2 minutes. Remove from the heat, cover, and allow to sit for at least 1 hour. Drain the chickpeas.

Combine the soaked and drained chickpeas, parsley, garlic, scallions, salt, spices, and lemon juice in a food processor. Pulse, scraping down the sides as necessary, until the chickpeas are finely minced but not puréed, and the mixture resembles small grains of couscous. When you gather a small amount of the mixture in your hand and squeeze, it should hold together. Scoop ¼ cup (64 g) of the chickpea mixture and form into a tight ball or oval with your hands. Place the chickpea patty on a plate. Repeat with the remaining mixture. You should be able to form 12 balls. Chill the formed patties for at least 15 minutes.

While the chickpea patties are chilling, make the Israeli salad. Combine the red peppers, cucumber, and red onion in a medium bowl. Drizzle the olive oil and vinegar over the vegetables and season with salt and pepper. Toss to combine. Cover and refrigerate the salad while you cook the falafel.

To cook the falafel, spray the basket of the air fryer with oil. Place half the falafel patties in the basket and spray the tops with oil. Cook at 400°F (200°C) until the tops are browned and crisp, about 8 minutes. Flip the falafel and spray the second side with oil. Cook until the second side is browned, 5 to 7 additional minutes. Remove the falafel and repeat with the remaining patties. Serve the falafel with the Israeli salad on the side.

Zucchini Rice Fritters

Turn leftover rice—whether homemade or takeout—into a satisfying vegetarian meal by adding fresh vegetables, herbs, and basic pantry ingredients and make a delicious fritter that cooks up brown and crispy in the air fryer. With zucchini, mint, and lemon, these rice fritters take their flavor inspiration from the Greek Isles. A little grated cheese makes them oh-so-gooey and nearly irresistible even for picky eaters.

The only binder for these fritters is beaten egg, so it is important that you firmly pack the rice mixture into a ball before dredging it in the bread crumbs. If you are having trouble getting your rice fritters to hold together, try chilling them for 15 minutes after forming.

3 cups (495 g) cooked rice

2 cups (240 g) grated cheese, such as Cheddar, Swiss, or Gruyère

1 medium zucchini, grated (about 2 cups)

4 scallions, white and light green parts only, sliced

¼ cup (24 g) tightly packed chopped fresh mint

3 eggs, beaten

Kosher salt and pepper to taste

1¼ cups (83 g) panko bread crumbs

Vegetable oil for spraying

Lemon wedges for serving

—
Makes 8 or 9 fritters, to serve 4

Combine the cooked rice, grated cheese, grated zucchini, scallions, and mint in a large bowl. Add the beaten eggs and season with salt and pepper. Stir to combine, making sure the egg is evenly distributed through the rice.

Spread the panko on a plate. Scoop out approximately ½ cup (82.5 g) of the rice mixture and form into a ball with your hands, pressing firmly to make the fritters as tight and well-packed as possible. Dredge the ball in the panko. Repeat with the remaining rice mixture. You should be able to make 8 or 9 fritters. Place half the fritters on a plate and chill until needed.

Spray the remaining half of the rice fritters and the basket of the air fryer with oil to prevent sticking. Place the fritters in the basket of the air fryer and cook at 400°F (200°C) until browned on all sides and cooked through, 10 to 12 minutes. Carefully remove the fritters to a platter and place the remaining fritters in the air fryer and cook in the same manner. Serve the rice fritters with lemon wedges for spritzing.

Zucchini, Spinach, and Feta Pancakes with Tzatziki

I always make some version of zucchini pancakes in the summer when zucchini is abundant and inexpensive at the farmers market. This version, with spinach, fresh herbs, and feta, is an especially satisfying and nutritious vegetarian meal. Because this dish is inspired by Greek flavors, I serve a refreshing cucumber tzatziki as an accompaniment. Use the same herbs, or combination of herbs, in the tzatziki as in the pancakes to simplify your shopping.

If I were making zucchini pancakes on the stove, I would not coat them with bread crumbs as I do here, but I discovered that the bread crumbs help prevent the pancakes from sticking to the air fryer as well as add a nice crunch.

TZATZIKI

1 English or hothouse cucumber

1 teaspoon kosher salt plus more to taste

1 cup (230 g) plain Greek yogurt, preferably full-fat

2 tablespoons (30 ml) freshly squeezed lemon juice

1 tablespoon (15 ml) extra-virgin olive oil

2 teaspoons chopped fresh herbs, such as mint, dill, and oregano

2 cloves garlic, minced

½ teaspoon black pepper

ZUCCHINI PANCAKES

3 small or 2 medium zucchini

1 teaspoon kosher salt

2 cups (60 g) tightly packed baby spinach leaves, sliced

3 scallions, white and light green parts only, sliced

2 cloves garlic, minced

4 ounces (115 g) Greek feta, crumbled (about ¾ cup)

2 tablespoons (10 g) chopped fresh herbs, such as mint, dill, or oregano

⅓ cup (42 g) all-purpose flour

½ teaspoon baking powder

1 teaspoon black pepper

2 eggs, beaten

1½ cups (75 g) panko bread crumbs

Vegetable oil for spraying

To make the tzatziki, coarsely grate the cucumber. Place the shreds in a colander and toss with 1 teaspoon of the salt. Allow to drain for at least 15 minutes. Pick up handfuls of cucumber and squeeze out the excess liquid. Place the drained shreds in a medium bowl. Add the yogurt, lemon juice, olive oil, herbs, garlic, and pepper. Stir to combine. Taste and add more salt if needed. Cover and chill for at least 1 hour to allow the flavors to develop.

To make the pancakes, coarsely grate the zucchini. Place the shreds in a colander and toss with the salt. Allow to drain for at least 15 minutes. Pick up handfuls of zucchini and squeeze out the excess liquid. Place the drained shreds in a medium bowl. Add the spinach, scallions, garlic, feta, herbs, flour, baking powder, and pepper and toss to combine. Pour the beaten eggs over the mixture and stir with a fork until thoroughly combined.

Spread the panko out on a plate. Scoop out approximately ½ cup (125 g) of the zucchini mixture and form into a 1-inch-thick (2.5 cm) oval patty with your hands. Dredge the patty in the panko. Spray both sides and the basket of the air fryer with oil. Carefully place the patty in the basket of the air fryer. Repeat twice more until you have 3 patties in the air fryer basket.

Cook at 375°F (190°C) until the top of the patty is browned and firm, 8 to 10 minutes. Using a silicone spatula, carefully flip the patties over and cook until the other side is well-browned, 4 to 6 minutes. Remove the cooked patties to a plate and repeat with the remaining batter, making 3 more patties.

Serve the zucchini pancakes hot or warm with tzatziki sauce on the side.

NOTE

For both the tzatziki sauce and the zucchini pancakes, I have you toss grated vegetables with salt and let them sit to draw out the moisture. Then I have you squeeze the liquid out of the grated shreds before using them in the recipe. This is because both cucumbers and zucchini contain a lot of water and could make the tzatziki sauce and the pancakes, respectively, soggy if we did not remove some of that liquid.

Cauliflower Steaks with Tahini Sauce

Cauliflower cut into flat "steaks" makes for a satisfying vegetarian meal any time of year. Because the core of the cauliflower holds these steaks together, you can only get two or three from each head. Save any remaining florets for another use, such as Korean Fried Cauliflower (page 74).

With the usual flour-egg-panko breading, these cruciferous steaks cook up crispy and crunchy on the outside and tender inside in only 15 minutes in the air fryer. I like to serve them with a lemony tahini sauce to give them a Middle Eastern flair, but they are pretty tasty with just a squeeze of lemon and a sprinkle of flat-leaf parsley. Sliced almonds or currants would also make a nice garnish.

TAHINI SAUCE

½ cup (120 g) tahini

½ cup (120 ml) freshly squeezed lemon juice

2 tablespoons (30 ml) extra-virgin olive oil

½ cup (120 ml) warm water

CAULIFLOWER STEAKS

2 heads cauliflower

1 cup (125 g) all-purpose flour

2 cups (100 g) panko bread crumbs

2 teaspoons thyme

2 teaspoons oregano

1 teaspoon kosher salt

1 teaspoon black pepper

2 eggs beaten with 2 tablespoons (30 ml) water

Vegetable oil for spraying

¼ cup (15 g) chopped flat-leaf parsley

Lemon wedges for serving

—

Serves 3 or 4

To make the tahini sauce, combine the tahini, lemon juice, and olive oil in a small bowl. Slowly whisk in the water until you reach the desired consistency, (You may not need the entire ½ cup.) Set aside.

To make the cauliflower steaks, remove the leaves and trim the stems of the cauliflower, leaving the cores intact. Stand the cauliflower on a cutting board. Using a large knife, slice off the rounded sides of the cauliflower, leaving the middle section still attached to the core. Slice this middle section into 2 or 3 flat "steaks," depending on the size of the cauliflower, 1 to 1½ inches (2.5 to 4 cm) thick.

Place the flour in a shallow dish or pie plate. In a separate shallow dish, combine the panko, thyme, oregano, salt, and pepper. Dredge 2 of the cauliflower steaks first in the flour, then the egg mixture, and finally the panko mixture, coating both sides. Remove to a plate.

Preheat the air fryer to 375°F (190°C). Spray both sides of the cauliflower steaks with oil and place in the basket of the air fryer. Cook for 15 to 17 minutes, flipping the steaks once halfway through, until the cauliflower is fork-tender and the breading is browned and crispy. Repeat with the remaining steaks. Drizzle tahini sauce over the steaks and serve with parsley and lemon wedges.

Kale and Mushroom Empanadas

Empanadas come in many forms, both baked and fried, and can be enjoyed as an appetizer, a snack, or a meal unto themselves. This vegetarian version features sautéed mushrooms and kale, so it feels both healthy and satisfying. Air-fried empanadas taste similar to a baked empanada but cook up in much less time and without having to heat up the whole house, which makes them an easy and convenient meal any time of the year.

Making empanadas from scratch is time-consuming and a true labor of love. To make these delightful turnovers more accessible for weeknight meals, I rely on frozen empanada discs which are easy to find in grocery stores with a good selection of Latin foods.

4 tablespoons (55 g) unsalted butter, divided

1 pound (455 g) mushrooms, sliced, divided

Kosher salt to taste

1 bunch kale, destemmed and cut into ribbons

3 cloves garlic, minced

Pinch red pepper flakes

Juice of 1 lemon

8 frozen empanada discs, thawed

Vegetable oil for spraying

—
Makes 8 empanadas, to serve 4

Melt 2 tablespoons (28 g) of butter in a large, deep skillet over medium-high heat. When the butter is foamy, add half the mushrooms and season with salt. Cook undisturbed for 2 minutes, then stir and cook for another minute or so. Turn the heat down to medium and sauté the mushrooms, stirring occasionally, until the liquid has evaporated and the mushrooms are browned, another 5 minutes. Remove the mushrooms to a paper towel–lined plate. Add the remaining butter and repeat with the remaining mushrooms. Set the mushrooms aside.

Add the kale to the same skillet and sauté until it begins to wilt, 2 to 3 minutes. Add the garlic and red pepper flakes and sauté for an additional minute. Add the lemon juice and season to taste with salt. Return the mushrooms to the skillet and stir to combine. Remove from the heat and allow the mixture to cool.

Remove 1 of the empanada wrappers and place it on a board. Place a heaping ¼ cup (36 g) of the mushroom-kale filling on 1 side of the empanada wrapper. Moisten the edges of the wrapper with a little water and fold the wrapper in half to form a half-moon shape. Press the dough closed around the filling and then crimp the edges of the dough with a fork to seal them shut. Place the filled empanada on a baking tray lined with parchment paper. (May be refrigerated, covered, at this point for up to several hours.)

Preheat the air fryer to 375°F (190°C). Spray the basket of the air fryer and the empanadas with oil. Working in 2 batches, place 4 empanadas in the basket of the air fryer. Cook for 8 minutes, then turn over the empanadas. Cook until the second side is firm and baked, another 5 to 7 minutes. Repeat with the second batch of empanadas. Serve immediately.

Loaded Baked Potatoes with Broccoli and Cheddar Cheese Sauce

One summer, my kids came home from camp and asked if we could have "baked potato bar" for dinner, like they do at camp. I probably pointed out that baked potatoes take over an hour to cook in the oven and that does not even include preheating time. When I learned that the air fryer can cook a baked potato to fluffy perfection in just 40 minutes, I became open to "baked potato bar" as a weeknight dinner option. My family enjoys this version with roasted broccoli—also cooked quickly in the air fryer—and cheese.

One could simply sprinkle grated cheese over the potatoes, but I think it is worth a few extra minutes to make a smooth, creamy Cheddar Cheese Sauce that coats the potatoes and broccoli and makes everyone want to scrape their plate clean. This recipe makes quite a bit, so you may have cheese sauce leftover—what a shame! Reheat it and toss with cooked pasta for a quick stovetop macaroni and cheese.

4 cups (284 g) small broccoli florets (from about 2 stalks)

2 tablespoons (30 ml) vegetable oil plus more for spraying

4 russet potatoes

CHEDDAR CHEESE SAUCE

4 tablespoons (55 g) unsalted butter

¼ cup (31 g) all-purpose flour

2 cups (480 ml) milk, warmed

1 teaspoon dry mustard

Dash Worcestershire sauce

Kosher salt and pepper to taste

12 ounces (340 g) sharp Cheddar cheese, grated

4 tablespoons (55 g) unsalted butter (optional)

—

Serves 4

Toss the broccoli florets with 2 tablespoons (30 ml) of oil in a bowl and set aside. Rub the skins of the potatoes with a small amount of oil and prick them all over with a fork. Place the potatoes in the basket of the air fryer and cook at 400°F (200°C) until you can easily pierce the potato with a knife, 40 to 50 minutes depending on the size of the potato.

While the potatoes are cooking, make the cheese sauce. Melt the butter in a large, heavy saucepan. Whisk in the flour and continue to cook over low heat, whisking constantly, for 4 to 5 minutes to cook the flour. Gradually add the milk to the saucepan, whisking constantly. Raise the heat to medium and cook until the sauce begins to thicken, about 3 to 5 minutes. Remove the saucepan from the heat and add the mustard, Worcestershire sauce, salt, and pepper. Gradually add the grated Cheddar in handfuls and stir to combine. Stir until the sauce is completely smooth. Keep warm while the potatoes continue to cook.

When the potatoes are cooked, remove them from the basket of the air fryer. Add the broccoli florets to the basket and cook until tender and the edges begin to brown, 8 to 10 minutes.

To serve, split open the top of each potato and squeeze the sides to open up the inside. If desired, add a pat of butter to each potato and season with salt and pepper. Divide the broccoli florets evenly among the 4 potatoes. Spoon cheese sauce over the broccoli and potatoes and serve immediately.

Sweet Potato and Farro Grain Bowls with Creamy Herb Dressing

Grain bowls are delicious and simple all-in-one meals that allow each member of the family to customize his or her own bowl. Typically composed of a grain, such as rice, farro, or barley, and topped with vegetables, protein, and dressing, grain bowls are an easy way to create a healthy meal that feels both hearty and light.

My favorite grain bowls typically start with farro, a protein- and fiber-packed ancient grain with a delicious nutty taste and slightly chewy texture. When cooked farro is toasted in the air fryer with a spritz of oil, the grains develop a crispy crust that perfectly complements their tender, nutty interior. Top the crispy farro with air-fried vegetables and your favorite vegetable protein, such as Orange and Rosemary Roasted Chickpeas (page 41), or a simple fried egg for a complete, one-dish meal.

CREAMY HERB DRESSING

½ cup (115 g) plain Greek yogurt

½ cup (8 g) fresh cilantro or (20 g) basil leaves

2 tablespoons (30 ml) extra-virgin olive oil

1 clove garlic, peeled

Juice of 1 lemon

½ teaspoon kosher salt

½ teaspoon cumin

GRAIN BOWLS

1 cup (110 g) diced sweet potatoes

2 cups (142 g) broccoli florets

1 teaspoon kosher salt, divided

2 teaspoons extra-virgin olive oil, divided

2 cups (330 g) cooked and cooled pearled farro (1 cup [195 g] of uncooked farro, prepared according to package directions)

½ small red onion, thinly sliced

1 small avocado, pitted and diced

Kosher salt and pepper to taste

—

Makes 2 grain bowls

To make the Creamy Herb Dressing, combine all dressing ingredients in a blender. Blend on medium speed until completely combined and smooth. If the dressing is too thick, add 1 to 2 tablespoons (15 to 30 ml) of water. (The dressing can be stored, covered, and refrigerated for up to 1 week.)

Combine the sweet potatoes, broccoli, and ½ teaspoon of the salt in a bowl with 1 teaspoon of the olive oil and toss to combine. Arrange the vegetables in a single layer in the basket of the air fryer and cook at 350°F (180°C) until the potatoes are golden brown and the broccoli is tender and starting to brown on the tops, about 8 minutes. Transfer the vegetables to a platter and keep warm.

Drizzle the cooked farro with the remaining teaspoon of olive oil and salt and toss to combine. Cut a small piece of parchment paper into a round to cover the bottom of the air fryer basket to prevent the farro grains from slipping through the basket holes. Add the farro to the basket and cook at 350°F (180°C) for 8 minutes, tossing gently halfway through to ensure that each grain is crisping, until the farro is crisp and golden.

Divide the farro between 2 bowls and top each with the sweet potatoes, broccoli, red onion, and avocado. Season with salt and pepper and drizzle with Creamy Herb Dressing. Serve warm or at room temperature.

Eggplant Parmesan

Eggplant Parmesan is typically layered and baked in a casserole, which means that the pieces of eggplant can get soggy and turn to mush. I prefer this version, where breaded eggplant cutlets are cooked in the air fryer until crispy then topped with a dollop of marinara sauce and grated cheese. The eggplant stays crisp while the sauce adds moisture and flavor and the cheese becomes gooey and melted.

Eggplant is beloved around the world for its meaty texture. This dish satisfies even the heartiest appetites while still being vegetarian.

MARINARA SAUCE

2 tablespoons (30 ml) extra-virgin olive oil

4 cloves garlic, minced

1 teaspoon kosher salt

½ teaspoon red pepper flakes

1 can (28 ounces, or 800 g) crushed tomatoes

1 teaspoon granulated sugar

EGGPLANT CUTLETS

4 small or baby eggplants

¾ cup (94 g) all-purpose flour

2 teaspoons kosher salt

1½ teaspoons freshly ground black pepper

1 cup (50 g) panko bread crumbs

1 cup (100 g) grated Parmesan cheese

2 eggs beaten with 2 tablespoons (30 ml) water

Vegetable oil for spraying

8 ounces (225 g) mozzarella cheese, grated

—
Serves 4

To make the marinara sauce, heat the olive oil in a medium saucepan over medium heat. Add the garlic, salt, and red pepper flakes and cook for 30 seconds to 1 minute, until the garlic is fragrant. Add the tomatoes and sugar and stir. Bring the sauce to a boil over high heat, then reduce the heat to low and simmer while you prepare the eggplant.

Trim the tops and bottoms off the eggplants. Cut each eggplant lengthwise into 3- or 4¼-inch (8 or 11 cm) slices. Whisk together the flour, salt, and pepper on a plate. Combine the panko and Parmesan cheese on a separate plate. Dredge 4 to 6 of the eggplant slices in the flour, tapping each one against the side of the bowl to remove any excess. Dip the slices in the egg mixture, allowing any excess to drip off. Then dredge the slices in the panko mixture. Place the breaded cutlets on a plate.

Spray the basket of the air fryer with oil. Arrange the breaded cutlets in a single layer in the air fryer basket and spray the tops with oil. Cook at 400°F (200°C) (375°F [190°C] for toaster oven–style machines) until the top side is browned and crisp, 5 to 7 minutes. While the first batch of cutlets is cooking, bread the remaining cutlets in the same manner.

Flip the cutlets and spray the second side with oil. Cook until the second side is browned, another 5 to 7 minutes. Carefully top each cutlet with 1 to 2 tablespoons of marinara sauce and 1 tablespoon of grated mozzarella. Cook for an additional 2 minutes until the mozzarella is melted and browned. Remove the cutlets and cook the second batch of breaded cutlets in the same manner. Repeat with the third batch of cutlets if necessary.

Serve the cutlets warm with pasta and the remaining marinara sauce on the side.

Paneer Tikka

Paneer is a firm, fresh Indian cheese that can be fried or grilled without melting or losing its shape. Like cheese curds, paneer has a bouncy texture and squeaks between your teeth. You have probably enjoyed it at Indian restaurants in dishes such as palak paneer. It is sold refrigerated, usually with the other cheeses, or sometimes frozen.

Because it holds its shape so well, paneer is a delight to cook in the air fryer with very little added fat. Here, we cube it and thread it on skewers with peppers and onions. A seasoned yogurt marinade adds flavor and gives the cooked paneer a nice char. Add some rice for a quick and easy vegetarian meal that everyone in the family will enjoy.

14 ounces (400 g) paneer

½ cup (115 g) plain yogurt

2 limes

2 cloves garlic, minced

1 tablespoon (15 ml) melted unsalted butter or vegetable oil

1 tablespoon (8 g) grated fresh ginger

1 teaspoon garam masala

1 teaspoon kosher salt

½ teaspoon cumin

¼ teaspoon turmeric

¼ teaspoon cayenne pepper

2 bell peppers, cored and cut into 1-inch (2.5 cm) squares

1 red onion, cut into wedges

Vegetable oil for spraying

—
Makes 8 skewers, to serve 4

Cut the paneer into 1-inch (2.5 cm) cubes. In a large bowl, whisk together the yogurt, zest and juice from 1 of the limes, garlic, butter, ginger, and spices. Add the paneer cubes to the yogurt mixture and toss gently to coat. Allow the paneer to marinate for 30 minutes.

Thread the paneer cubes, bell pepper pieces, and onion wedges onto metal skewers designed for the air fryer or bamboo skewers cut to fit an air fryer. (If using bamboo skewers, soak them in water for 30 minutes prior to use.)

Spray the basket of the air fryer with oil. Working in batches, place 4 of the skewers in the air fryer basket and spray with oil. Cook at 375°F (190°C) for 10 minutes, turning the skewers once. Repeat with the remaining skewers. Serve the paneer tikka hot with rice and lime wedges for spritzing.

CHAPTER 4
Chicken, Turkey, and Duck

Tropical Glazed Chicken Salad with Mangoes
and Candied Pecans 84

Chicken Parmesan 85

Buttermilk Fried Chicken and Waffles 86

Piri-Piri Chicken Thighs 90

Mushroom Turkey Burgers 88

Israeli Chicken Schnitzel 91

Tandoori-Style Chicken Skewers 92

General Tso's Chicken 94

Orange-Glazed Duck Breast
with Apples 95

Tropical Glazed Chicken Salad with Mangoes and Candied Pecans

This main-course salad is a light yet satisfying meal that comes together in the time that it takes the chicken breasts to cook in the air fryer. Peach-mango preserves glaze the chicken breasts and then appear again in the sweet-tart salad dressing. Ataulfo mangoes, sometimes called Champagne or honey mangoes, hail from Mexico and are available from February through August. You will love their buttery, smooth texture and honey-sweet taste in this salad.

While boneless, skinless breasts can turn out tough and rubbery when cooked in the oven, they stay moist and juicy when cooked in the intense heat and fast-moving air of the air fryer, making them a staple for quick and easy weeknight dinners.

DRESSING

2 tablespoons (40 g) peach-mango preserves

2 tablespoons (30 ml) white wine or champagne vinegar

2 tablespoons (30 ml) freshly squeezed lime juice

1 tablespoon (15 g) Dijon mustard

¼ cup (60 ml) extra-virgin olive oil

SALAD

1 pound (455 g) boneless, skinless chicken breasts (2 breasts, each weighing 8 ounces [225 g])

1 teaspoon vegetable oil

Kosher salt and pepper to taste

2 tablespoons (40 g) peach-mango preserves

5 ounces (140 g) mixed baby greens

2 ripe Ataulfo mangoes, peeled and cut into cubes

½ red onion, shaved

2 cups (200 g) Sweet and Smoky Candied Pecans (page 63)

—
Serves 2 to 4

To make the dressing, combine the peach-mango preserves, vinegar, lime juice, and mustard together in a small bowl and whisk to combine. While whisking, slowly pour in the olive oil and continue to whisk until emulsified. Set aside.

To cook the chicken, pat the chicken breasts dry with paper towels and brush with oil. Season well with salt and pepper. Preheat the air fryer to 400°F (200°C) for 2 minutes. Add the chicken to the air fryer basket, top side down. Cook the chicken on the first side for 4 minutes. While the chicken is cooking, microwave the preserves for 30 seconds to make them easier to spread. Flip the chicken and brush the top side with the preserves. Return to the air fryer and cook for an additional 8 to 12 minutes until cooked through and the internal temperature reaches 165°F (74°C). Remove the chicken from the air fryer and allow it to rest.

While the chicken is resting, assemble the salad. Place the mixed baby greens in a wide, shallow serving bowl. Top with mango and shaved red onion. Dress the salad and toss gently to combine. Slice the chicken on the diagonal and add it to the salad. Add the candied pecans. Serve immediately.

Chicken Parmesan

Chicken parmesan is my husband's favorite dinner. He loves this air fryer version, which is crispy and delicious but never greasy. Hand-filleted or "thin-cut" chicken breasts are perfectly sized for this recipe. If using regular chicken breasts, simply slice each breast in half crosswise to create thin cutlets that will cook quickly and evenly.

When buying Parmesan cheese, it is worthwhile to seek out real Parmigiano-Reggiano imported from Italy. You can identify it through the pin dots in the cheese's rind, which also has the name stamped on it in black. Domestic Parmesan, while less expensive, lacks the complexity and depth of flavor of real, imported Parmigiano-Reggiano.

1 egg

1 tablespoon (14 g) mayonnaise

1 cup (50 g) panko bread crumbs

½ cup (75 g) freshly grated Parmesan cheese

1 teaspoon Italian seasoning

1 pound (455 g) boneless, skinless hand-filleted chicken breasts or regular breasts sliced in half crosswise to create 4 thin breasts

Vegetable oil for spraying

¼ cup (61 g) Marinara Sauce (page 80)

6 tablespoons (45 g) grated mozzarella cheese

Mix the egg and mayonnaise in a shallow bowl until smooth. In another bowl, combine the panko, Parmesan cheese, and Italian seasoning. Dip each piece of chicken in the mayonnaise mixture, shaking off any excess, then dredge in the panko mixture until both sides are coated. Place the breaded chicken on a plate or rack.

Preheat the air fryer to 350°F (180°C) for 3 minutes. Spray the basket of the air fryer with oil and place 2 pieces of chicken in the basket. Spray the chicken cutlets with oil. Cook the cutlets for 6 minutes, then turn them over. Top each piece of chicken with 1 tablespoon (15 g) of marinara sauce and 1½ tablespoons (11 g) of grated mozzarella cheese. Cook the chicken until the cheese is melted, about 3 additional minutes.

Remove the cooked chicken to a serving dish and keep warm. Cook the remaining pieces of chicken in the same manner. Serve warm with pasta on the side.

Buttermilk Fried Chicken and Waffles

This meal is all about having fun with your countertop appliances. Make fried chicken tenders in the air fryer and tasty buttermilk waffles in the waffle iron. Serve the chicken atop the waffles and pass the maple syrup and hot sauce!

The hardest thing about this recipe is timing the two elements. The chicken takes 15 to 20 minutes in the air fryer and needs only to be flipped once. Making waffles in a waffle iron, on the other hand, requires your constant attention. If you are good at multitasking, I recommend making the waffles while the chicken cooks. If not, make the chicken first and keep it warm in the air fryer at a low temperature while you make the waffles.

FRIED CHICKEN

4 small boneless, skinless chicken breasts totaling approximately 2 pounds (910 g)

½ cup (63 g) all-purpose flour

1 teaspoon kosher salt

½ teaspoon cayenne pepper

1 egg

2 tablespoons (30 ml) buttermilk

Dash hot sauce

1½ cups (75 g) panko bread crumbs

Vegetable oil for spraying

BUTTERMILK WAFFLES

1¾ cups (219 g) all-purpose flour

2 teaspoons baking powder

1 teaspoon granulated sugar

1 teaspoon baking soda

1 teaspoon kosher salt

1¾ cups (420 ml) buttermilk

2 eggs

½ cup (112 g, or 1 stick) unsalted butter, melted and cooled

Maple syrup or honey to serve

—
Serves 4

To make the chicken, cut each chicken breast in half lengthwise to make 2 long chicken tenders. Whisk together the flour, salt, and cayenne pepper on a large plate. Beat the egg with the buttermilk and hot sauce in a large, shallow bowl. Place the panko in a separate shallow bowl or pie plate.

Dredge the chicken tenders in the flour, shaking off any excess, then dip them in the egg mixture. Dredge the chicken tenders in the panko, making sure to coat them completely. Shake off any excess panko. Place the battered chicken tenders on a plate.

Preheat the air fryer to 375°F (190°C). Spray the basket lightly with oil. Arrange half the chicken tenders in the basket of the air fryer and spray the tops with oil. Cook at 375°F (190°C) until the top side of the tenders is browned and crispy, 8 to 10 minutes. Flip the tenders and spray the second side with oil. Cook until the second side is browned and crispy and the internal temperature reaches 165°F (71°C), another 8 to 10 minutes. Remove the first batch of tenders and keep it warm. Cook the second batch in the same manner.

While the tenders are cooking, make the waffles. In a large bowl, whisk together the flour, baking powder, sugar, baking soda, and salt. In a separate bowl, whisk together the buttermilk, eggs, and melted butter, reserving a small amount of butter to brush on the waffle iron. Add the wet ingredients to the dry ingredients and stir with a fork until just combined. Allow the batter to rest for at least 5 minutes. Brush the waffle iron with reserved melted butter and preheat according to the manufacturer's instructions. Scoop ⅓ to ½ cup (85 to 125 g) of batter into each grid of the waffle iron and cook according to your waffle iron's instructions. (You should be able to make 8 waffles.)

To serve, place 2 chicken tenders on top of 1 or 2 waffles, depending on the person's appetite. Serve with maple syrup or honey and additional hot sauce.

Mushroom Turkey Burgers

Too often, turkey burgers are dry and tasteless, making you wish you had just made regular hamburgers. To combat that, I blend dark-meat ground turkey—much more flavorful than ground turkey breast—with chopped sautéed mushrooms, which add both moisture and flavor to the meat. Sautéing the mushrooms adds an extra step, but the results are worth it. Fortunately, the burgers themselves cook up quickly in the air fryer.

If your family likes cheeseburgers, after the burgers are cooked, add a slice of cheese to each burger, pressing down to ensure that it doesn't blow off in the air fryer, and cook for an additional minute.

1 tablespoon (14 g) unsalted butter or (15 ml) extra-virgin olive oil

8 ounces (225 g) sliced mushrooms

1½ teaspoons kosher salt, divided

1 pound (455 g) ground dark-meat turkey

½ onion, grated

1 tablespoon (15 ml) Worcestershire sauce

1 teaspoon garlic powder

1 teaspoon black pepper

Vegetable oil for spraying

4 hamburger buns

—
Serves 4

Heat the butter in a large, heavy skillet over medium-high heat. Add the mushrooms and arrange in a single layer. Cook the mushrooms without stirring for 2 minutes. Stir and cook for 1 to 2 minutes more. Reduce the heat and continue to sauté until the mushrooms are no longer giving off liquid, about 5 minutes. Season with ½ teaspoon salt and remove from the heat. Finely mince the mushrooms or chop them in a food processor.

In a large bowl, combine the minced mushrooms, turkey, onion, Worcestershire, garlic powder, and remaining salt and pepper. Divide the mixture into 4 equal patties and using your finger, create a small depression in the middle of each patty.

Spray the patties and the basket of the air fryer with oil to prevent sticking. Cook the patties at 375°F (190°C) until browned and the internal temperature registers 165°F (71°C), about 15 minutes. Remove the burgers from the air fryer. Serve on buns garnished with your favorite burger toppings.

Piri-Piri Chicken Thighs

Piri-piri, sometimes spelled peri-peri, is a spicy sauce made from the bird's-eye chile pepper, which Portuguese traders brought from the Americas to colonies in Africa—modern-day Angola and Mozambique. Piri-piri sauce combines the fruitiness and heat of the bird's-eye chile with garlic, onions, lemon juice, and herbs to make a complex, flavorful hot sauce that is magical on chicken.

You should be able to find piri-piri in the hot sauce aisle of your grocery store or, at worst, online. Here, the chicken is marinated in the piri-piri sauce prior to cooking and then the marinade is cooked (to kill any germs from the raw chicken) and thickened to make a glaze that coats the chicken at the very end of cooking. The result is beautifully burnished, spicy chicken thighs that are anything but ordinary weekday fare. Serve alongside rice pilaf for a South African–inspired meal.

¼ cup (60 ml) piri-piri sauce

1 tablespoon (15 ml) freshly squeezed lemon juice

2 tablespoons (30 g) brown sugar, divided

2 cloves garlic, minced

1 tablespoon (15 ml) extra-virgin olive oil

4 bone-in, skin-on chicken thighs, each weighing approximately 7 to 8 ounces (195 to 225 g)

½ teaspoon cornstarch

—

Serves 4

To make the marinade, whisk together the piri-piri sauce, lemon juice, 1 tablespoon (9.5 g) of the brown sugar, and the garlic in a small bowl. While whisking, slowly pour in the oil in a steady stream and continue to whisk until emulsified. Using a skewer, poke holes in the chicken thighs and place them in a small glass dish. Pour the marinade over the chicken and turn the thighs to coat them with the sauce. Cover the dish and refrigerate for at least 15 minutes and up to 1 hour.

Preheat the air fryer to 375°F (190°C). Remove the chicken thighs from the dish, reserving the marinade, and place them skin side down in the basket of the air fryer. Cook until the internal temperature reaches 165°F (71°C), 15 to 20 minutes. Meanwhile, whisk the remaining tablespoon (15 g) of brown sugar and the cornstarch into the marinade and microwave it on high power for 1 minute until it is bubbling and thickened to a glaze.

Once the chicken is cooked, turn the thighs over and brush them with the glaze. Cook for a few additional minutes until the glaze browns and begins to char in spots. Remove the chicken to a platter and serve with additional piri-piri sauce, if desired.

Israeli Chicken Schnitzel

Crispy, juicy chicken schnitzel is practically ubiquitous in Israel, where it is a favorite with adults and kids alike. (Turkey schnitzel is quite popular as well.) In fact, this dish has become so associated with Israel in diners' minds that many Israeli restaurants in America have chicken schnitzel on their menus right next to the falafel and hummus.

This simple, tasty dish of chicken breast that is pounded thin so it is big enough to cover a dinner plate before being breaded and fried should be a favorite with Americans as well—especially because the air fryer makes it healthier and less messy than the pan-fried version. Serve chicken schnitzel with lots of lemon wedges for spritzing.

2 large boneless, skinless chicken breasts, each weighing about 1 pound (455 g)

1 cup (125 g) all-purpose flour

2 teaspoons garlic powder

2 teaspoons kosher salt

1 teaspoon black pepper

1 teaspoon paprika

2 eggs beaten with 2 tablespoons (30 ml) water

2 cups (100 g) panko bread crumbs

Vegetable oil for spraying

Lemon for serving

—
Serves 4

Place 1 of the chicken breasts between 2 pieces of plastic wrap. Use a mallet or a rolling pin to pound the chicken until it is ¼ inch (6 mm) thick. Set aside. Repeat with the second breast. Whisk together the flour, garlic powder, salt, pepper, and paprika on a large plate. Place the panko in a separate shallow bowl or pie plate.

Dredge 1 of the chicken breasts in the flour, shaking off any excess, then dip it in the egg mixture. Dredge the chicken breast in the panko, making sure to coat it completely. Shake off any excess panko. Place the battered chicken breast on a plate. Repeat with the second chicken breast.

Spray the basket of the air fryer with oil. Place 1 of the battered chicken breasts in the basket and spray the top with oil. Cook at 375°F (190°C) until the top is browned, about 5 minutes. Flip the chicken and spray the second side with oil. Cook until the second side is browned and crispy and the internal temperature reaches 165°F (71°C). Remove the first chicken breast from the air fryer and repeat the process with the second chicken breast. Serve hot with plenty of lemons for squeezing.

Tandoori-Style Chicken Skewers

Technically speaking, tandoori chicken is chicken that has been marinated in a mixture of yogurt and spices and cooked in a super-hot clay tandoor oven. That is why I call this dish of chicken marinated in a mixture of yogurt and spices and cooked in the air fryer *tandoori-style* chicken. But no matter what you call it, everyone will enjoy these flavorful, juicy chicken skewers, which cook in just 10 minutes.

In earlier times, the yogurt in the tandoori marinade not only flavored the chicken but also tenderized it. The chicken we buy today is already plenty tender, which means the marinating time can be as short as 20 minutes—just long enough to flavor the chicken. Whip up a quick-cooking vegetable side dish, and dinner is on the table in a flash. Some coconut rice or warm naan bread would round out the meal perfectly.

1½ pounds (680 g) hand-filleted boneless, skinless chicken breast or regular boneless, skinless chicken breast pounded to ¼-inch (6 mm) thickness

4 cloves garlic, peeled

1 piece (1 inch [2.5 cm]) fresh ginger, peeled

1 cup (230 g) plain yogurt, preferably full fat

1 tablespoon (6 g) Tandoori Spice Mix (page 53)

1 teaspoon kosher salt

Juice and zest of 1 lime plus more for serving

Vegetable oil for spraying

—
Serves 4

Cut the chicken breast into strips approximately 1 inch (2.5 cm) wide and place in a glass baking dish. Mince the garlic and ginger together very finely to form a chunky paste. Whisk the garlic-ginger paste with the yogurt, spice mix, salt, and lime zest and juice in a medium bowl until combined. Pour the yogurt mixture into the baking dish with the chicken and turn the chicken pieces until they are coated. Cover the dish and refrigerate at least 20 minutes and up to 6 hours.

Preheat the air fryer to 400°F (200°C). If desired, thread half the chicken pieces onto metal skewers designed for the air fryer and place them on a rack. Alternatively, you can simply spray the air fryer basket with oil to prevent sticking and lay half the chicken pieces in the basket. Cook at 400°F (200°C) for 10 minutes, turning once halfway through. Repeat with the remaining chicken pieces.

Serve immediately with additional lime wedges for spritzing.

General Tso's Chicken

Who doesn't love crunchy, spicy-sweet General Tso's Chicken? I never go out for Chinese food without ordering some. This air-fried version has all the crunch and spicy flavor of the original but with a fraction of the fat and calories, especially because we use boneless, skinless chicken breast for the meat. Do not be tempted to dredge all of the chicken in the cornstarch at once. It will start to get soggy while it sits. Instead, work in batches and dredge the chicken pieces in cornstarch right before cooking for best results.

Serve with rice and steamed broccoli and remind everyone that the red chiles are not to be eaten!

2 pounds (910 g) boneless, skinless chicken breast, cut into bite-size cubes

½ cup (120 ml) soy sauce, divided

½ cup (120 ml) mirin or rice wine, divided

½ cup (65 g) plus ½ tablespoon (4 g) cornstarch

2 tablespoons (30 ml) vegetable or canola oil plus additional oil for spraying

2 cloves garlic, minced

1 tablespoon (8 g) grated fresh ginger

12 dried red chiles

¼ cup (60 ml) rice vinegar

¼ cup (50 g) granulated sugar

2 teaspoons hoisin sauce (optional)

2 scallions, white and light green part only, sliced

1 teaspoon sesame seeds

—
Serves 4

Toss the chicken with ¼ cup (60 ml) of the soy sauce and ¼ cup (60 ml) of the mirin in a glass bowl or baking dish. Cover and refrigerate for at least 15 and up to 30 minutes.

Spread ½ cup (65 g) of cornstarch on a plate. Take 2 pieces of chicken and dredge them in the cornstarch, then tap them against each other to remove any excess. Repeat until you have dredged one-third of the chicken in the cornstarch. Spray the basket of the air fryer with oil. Arrange the dredged chicken pieces in the basket in a single layer. Spray with oil. Cook at 400°F (200°C) for 8 minutes, turning once, spraying with additional oil if there are dry patches of cornstarch. Set aside.

While the first batch of chicken is cooking, dredge the second third of the chicken in the cornstarch. Spray the basket of the air fryer with oil and cook the second batch of chicken in the same manner. While the second batch is cooking, dredge the remaining chicken in the cornstarch. Cook the last third of the chicken in the same manner as the others. Set the cooked chicken aside.

Whisk together the remaining ½ tablespoon (4 g) of cornstarch with ½ tablespoon (7.5 ml) of water to create a slurry and set aside. Heat the 2 tablespoons (30 ml) of oil in a large, deep skillet over medium heat. Add the garlic, ginger, and dried red chiles and sauté for 1 minute until fragrant but not browned. Add the remaining soy sauce, mirin, rice vinegar, sugar, and hoisin sauce, if using, and bring to a boil, stirring to dissolve the sugar. Add the cornstarch slurry and cook until the mixture begins to thicken, 1 to 2 minutes.

Add the chicken to the sauce in the pan and toss to coat. Cook until the chicken is heated through. Remove the chicken and sauce to a platter and garnish with scallions and sesame seeds. Serve immediately.

Orange-Glazed Duck Breast with Apples

Glazed duck breast with apples has all the hallmarks of an elegant, special-occasion dinner, but, remarkably, it comes together in less than 30 minutes in the air fryer. Perfect for when that special occasion—be it a birthday, anniversary, or Valentine's Day—falls during the week. A simple rice pilaf and a special dessert—perhaps Caramelized Pineapple with Mint and Lime (page 138)—would complete this meal beautifully.

Duck is an excellent meat for the air fryer because there is so much fat in the skin and you do not need to add any oil or butter. Scoring the skin will help render the duck fat so it can flavor the meat. Just take care not to cut through to the flesh. And be sure to clean the air fryer well after cooking the duck.

1 pound (455 g) duck breasts (2 to 3 breasts)

Kosher salt and pepper

Juice and zest of 1 orange

¼ cup (85 g) honey

2 sprigs thyme plus more for garnish

2 firm tart apples, such as Fuji

—

Serves 2 or 3

Pat the duck breasts dry and, using a sharp knife, make 3 to 4 shallow, diagonal slashes in the skin. Turn the breasts and score the skin on the diagonal in the opposite direction to create a cross-hatch pattern. Season well with salt and pepper.

Preheat the air fryer to 400°F (200°C). Place the duck breasts skin side up in the basket of the air fryer. Cook for 8 minutes, then flip and cook for 4 more minutes on the second side.

While the duck is cooking, prepare the sauce. Combine the orange juice and zest, honey, and thyme in a small saucepan. Bring to a boil, stirring to dissolve the honey, then reduce the heat and simmer until thickened. Core the apples and cut into quarters. Cut each quarter into 3 or 4 slices depending on the size.

After the duck has cooked on both sides, turn it skin side up and brush the skin with the orange-honey glaze. Cook for 1 more minute. Remove the duck breasts to a cutting board and allow to rest.

Toss the apple slices with the remaining orange-honey sauce in a medium bowl. Arrange the apples in a single layer in the basket of the air fryer. Cook for 10 minutes while the duck breast rests. Slice the duck breasts on the bias and divide them and the apples among 2 or 3 plates. Serve warm, garnished with additional thyme.

Beef, Lamb, and Pork

Country-Fried Steak with Onion Gravy   98

Argentinian Beef Empanadas   100

Lamb Kofta with Tzatziki   101

Perfect Spice-Rubbed Ribeye for One (or Two)   102

Sicilian Stuffed Peppers   103

Cumin-Crusted Pork Tenderloin and Potatoes   104

Sonoran Hot Dogs   106

Teriyaki-Glazed Baby Back Ribs   107

Monte Cristo Sandwich   108

Country-Fried Steak with Onion Gravy

Country-fried steak, also known as chicken-fried steak, is the very definition of a guilty pleasure. Unless, of course, you make it in the air fryer, in which case it is nearly guilt free. The air fryer turns out a flavorful, tender steak with a crispy coating that rivals any diner's version of this iconic dish and without any oil. I recommend starting with tenderized cube steaks for best results.

The only thing better than country-fried steak is country-fried steak smothered in gravy. So if you have a few extra minutes, before cooking the steaks, make a quick onion gravy with basic pantry ingredients. If you have ever been intimidated by making gravy, this no-fail method will turn you into a gravy expert.

ONION GRAVY

1 tablespoon (14 g) unsalted butter

1 tablespoon (15 ml) vegetable oil

1 yellow onion, thinly sliced

Kosher salt and pepper to taste

2 tablespoons (16 g) all-purpose flour

2 cups (480 ml) chicken broth, warmed

½ teaspoon Worcestershire sauce

COUNTRY-FRIED STEAK

½ cup (63 g) all-purpose flour

1 teaspoon kosher salt

½ teaspoon black pepper

½ teaspoon onion powder

½ teaspoon garlic powder

1 egg

¼ cup (60 ml) milk

1½ cups (75 g) panko bread crumbs

4 cube steaks (4 ounces, or 115 g each)

—

Serves 4

To make the onion gravy, melt the butter and oil in a large skillet over medium heat. Add the onion and season with salt and pepper. Sauté the onion over medium to medium-low heat, stirring occasionally, until softened and browned, approximately 15 minutes. Sprinkle the flour over the onion and stir to combine. Sauté for an additional 2 minutes until the flour smells toasty. While stirring, slowly pour in the warm chicken broth and Worcestershire sauce. Use your spoon to deglaze the pan by scraping up any brown bits that have accumulated on the bottom. Simmer the gravy until thickened, stirring frequently to prevent scorching, 8 to 10 minutes. Taste and adjust the seasoning. Keep warm over a very low flame while you make the steaks.

To make the steaks, whisk together the flour, salt, pepper, and onion and garlic powders in a shallow pie plate or dish. In a second shallow dish, beat together the egg and the milk. Spread the panko on a third plate or dish. Dredge a cube steak in the flour, shaking off any excess. Next, coat the steak with the egg-milk mixture. Finally, dredge the steak in the panko, shaking off any excess. Place the coated steak on a rack or plate. Repeat with the remaining steaks.

Preheat the air fryer to 375°F (190°C). Place 2 of the steaks in the air fryer and cook for 12 to 14 minutes, flipping once halfway through, until browned and crispy. Remove the steaks and keep warm while you cook the remaining 2 steaks in the same manner. Serve the steaks topped with onion gravy.

Argentinian Beef Empanadas

The combination of beef, raisins, green olives, and hard-boiled eggs is the classic filling for an Argentinian beef empanada. The sweet raisins and the briny olives are the perfect foil for the fattiness of the meat. Frozen empanada wrappers, which cook up crisp and flaky, turn this one-time labor of love into an accessible weeknight dinner. Leftover empanadas make a great brown-bag lunch the next day.

2 tablespoons (28 g) unsalted butter

1 yellow onion, diced

1 red bell pepper, diced

1 pound (455 g) ground beef

1½ tablespoons (10.5 g) cumin

1 tablespoon (7 g) paprika

1 teaspoon oregano

1 teaspoon kosher salt, plus more for seasoning

⅓ cup (50 g) raisins

½ cup (50 g) green olives, sliced

2 hard-boiled eggs, sliced

Juice of 1 lime

1 package (12 ounces, or 340 g) frozen empanada discs, thawed

Vegetable oil for spraying

—

Makes 10 to 12 empanadas, to serve 4

To make the empanada filling, heat the butter in a large, deep skillet over medium heat. When the butter is foamy, add the onion, season with salt, and sauté for 5 minutes. Add the bell pepper and sauté an additional 3 minutes. Add the ground beef and spices and cook, stirring, until the meat is no longer pink. Remove from the heat. Drain any accumulated fat from the pan. Add the raisins, green olives, and eggs, stir to combine, and allow to cool to room temperature. Add the lime juice and stir to combine. Taste and adjust the seasoning, adding more salt as necessary.

Remove 1 of the empanada wrappers from the package and place it on a board. Using a rolling pin, roll the wrapper out in each direction so that it is slightly larger. Place a heaping ¼ cup (50 g) of the beef filling on 1 side of the empanada wrapper. Moisten the edges of the wrapper with a little water and fold the wrapper in half to form a half-moon shape. Press the dough closed around the filling and then crimp the edges of the dough with a fork to seal them shut. Place the filled empanada on a baking tray lined with parchment paper. Repeat with the remaing wrappers and filling. (May be refrigerated, covered, at this point for up to several hours.)

Preheat the air fryer to 375°F (190°C). Spray the basket of the air fryer and the empanadas with oil. Working in 2 batches, place 5 empanadas in the basket of the air fryer. Cook for 8 minutes, then turn the empanadas over. Cook until the second side is firm and baked, another 5 to 7 minutes. Repeat with the second batch of empanadas. Serve immediately.

Lamb Kofta with Tzatziki

Americans eat far less lamb than their counterparts in Europe, Australia, and New Zealand. Indeed, Americans consume just 1 pound of lamb per person per year compared to more than 60 pounds of beef. That's a shame, because lamb, which is mostly grass fed, is both flavorful and healthy, and is especially rich in omega-3 fatty acids.

Ground lamb is milder in flavor and less expensive than lamb chops or leg of lamb, so it is a perfect entry point. These ground lamb patties, known as *kofta* in the Middle East and North Africa, are usually grilled, but it is so easy and convenient to cook them in the air fryer. They take just 10 minutes to come out tender and juicy. Serve them with refreshing Tzatziki (page 72) and fresh pita bread or rice pilaf for a Mediterranean-inspired dinner.

1 pound (455 g) ground lamb

½ onion, grated

¼ cup (15 g) chopped fresh flat-leaf parsley, mint, or a combination

1 teaspoon kosher salt

½ teaspoon cumin

½ teaspoon coriander

½ teaspoon paprika

¼ teaspoon allspice

¼ teaspoon cinnamon

Vegetable oil for spraying

Tzatziki (page 72) for serving

—
Serves 4

Combine the lamb, onion, herbs, salt, and spices in a medium bowl and mix thoroughly. Form the lamb mixture into 8 equal, tightly packed patties. Place the patties on a plate, cover, and refrigerate for at least 30 minutes and up to 8 hours.

To cook the lamb kofta, preheat the air fryer to 400°F (200°C). Spray the air fryer basket with oil. Working in 2 batches, if necessary so as not to overcrowd the air fryer basket, arrange the patties in a single layer. Cook until the internal temperature reaches 145°F (63°C), about 10 minutes, flipping the patties once halfway through cooking.

Remove the patties to a paper towel–lined plate to absorb excess oil. Serve the patties warm with Tzatziki.

Perfect Spice-Rubbed Ribeye for One (or Two)

Do you ever need to cook just one steak? Of course you do. Perhaps you are preparing a vegetarian feast, but there's that one person in your family who is strictly meat-and-potatoes. Or perhaps you are on your own for the evening and have decided to treat yourself to a steak dinner. Whatever the reason, cooking just one steak is easy to do using your air fryer. Don't bother heating up the grill!

When you coat the steak with a dry spice rub that contains a hint of brown sugar, the outside caramelizes while the inside remains pink and juicy. I like a Middle Eastern–inspired rub with cumin and coriander, but you can experiment with different spice combinations or just stick with sugar, salt, and pepper. The most important thing, however, is to allow the steak to come to room temperature before cooking. Sliced and served over greens, this steak also makes an elegant light meal for two.

¾ to 1 pound (340 to 455 g) boneless ribeye, at least 1 inch (2.5 cm) thick

1½ teaspoons kosher salt

1 teaspoon brown sugar

1 teaspoon coarsely ground black pepper

½ teaspoon cumin

½ teaspoon coriander

¼ teaspoon hot paprika

Vegetable oil for spraying

—
Serves 1 or 2

Pat the steak dry with paper towels. Allow the steak to sit for at least 20 minutes until it is at room temperature. Whisk together the salt, sugar, and spices. Rub both sides of the steak with the spice mixture.

Preheat the air fryer to 400°F (200°C). Spray the air fryer basket with oil. Place the steak in the air fryer basket. Cook undisturbed at 400°F (200°C) for 8 minutes. After 8 minutes, begin checking the internal temperature using a meat thermometer. For medium-rare, cook to 140°F (60°C); for medium, 155°F (68°C). Continue cooking the steak until you achieve the desired doneness. Allow the meat to rest for 5 minutes before slicing and serving.

Sicilian Stuffed Peppers

Stuffed peppers is a dish with a lot of parts. You have to sauté aromatics, brown meat, and cook rice for the filling before cooking the stuffed peppers in the oven, which can take up to an hour. At least the air fryer makes quick work of the last step—the peppers become fork-tender in under 20 minutes. As for the filling, think of stuffed peppers whenever you have leftover rice in the house. After that, the whole thing comes together quite quickly.

Ground beef with pine nuts, raisins, and a splash of vinegar may seem like a strange combination, but this mix of sweet and sour flavors is typical of Sicilian cuisine, and the flavors balance each other nicely.

2 tablespoons (30 ml) extra-virgin olive oil

1 yellow onion, diced

3 cloves garlic, minced

¾ pound (340 g) ground beef

2 teaspoons kosher salt

Pinch red pepper flakes

2 medium tomatoes or 1 large tomato

¼ cup (35 g) pine nuts

¼ cup (35 g) raisins

3 tablespoons (45 ml) red wine vinegar

1 cup (165 g) cooked rice

4 red bell peppers

Vegetable oil for spraying

1 cup (150 g) grated mozzarella cheese

—

Serves 4

Heat the olive oil in a large, deep skillet over medium heat. When the oil is shimmering, add the onion and sauté until softened, about 5 minutes. Add the garlic and sauté for an additional minute. Add the ground beef, salt, and red pepper flakes and cook until the meat is no longer pink, about 6 minutes. If the meat has given off a lot of grease, carefully remove it from the pan with a spoon.

Slice off the stem end of the tomatoes and grate them using the coarse side of a box grater. Discard the skin. Add the tomato pulp, pine nuts, raisins, and vinegar to the meat mixture and sauté a few additional minutes to thicken. Add the cooked rice and stir to combine. Remove from the heat and set aside.

If you have a drawer-style air fryer with a deep basket, cut off the top third of the peppers and remove the seeds and inner membranes. Divide the meat mixture evenly among the 4 peppers. Place the tops back on the peppers and place them carefully in the basket of the air fryer. Spray or brush the outsides and tops of the peppers with oil. Cook at 375°F (190°C) for 15 minutes, rotating the peppers halfway through. Remove the tops and add ¼ cup (37.5 g) grated mozzarella to each pepper. Cook until the cheese is melted and browned, about 4 minutes.

If you have a toaster oven–style air fryer, cut the peppers in half through the stem. Brush the bottoms of the peppers with oil. Arrange the peppers in a single layer in the basket of the air fryer. Divide the meat mixture evenly among the pepper halves. Cook at 350°F (180°C) until the peppers are tender, about 10 minutes. Sprinkle 2 tablespoons (19 g) of grated cheese on top of each pepper half and cook until the cheese is melted and brown, 2 to 3 minutes. Serve immediately.

Cumin-Crusted Pork Tenderloin and Potatoes

This easy, spice-crusted pork tenderloin with potatoes is an all-in-one dinner that is ideal for busy weekday evenings. The tenderloin cooks in just 20 minutes in the air fryer and the potatoes cook while the pork rests. Whip up a green salad and you have a complete meal that is ready in under 30 minutes.

3 tablespoons (21 g) ground cumin

1 teaspoon chili powder

1 teaspoon kosher salt

¼ teaspoon black pepper

2 cloves garlic, minced

1 pound (455 g) pork tenderloin, cut into 2 pieces

Vegetable oil for spraying

1 pound (455 g) Yukon gold potatoes, quartered

1 tablespoon (15 ml) extra-virgin olive oil

—
Serves 4 to 6

Combine the spices and garlic in a small bowl. Transfer 1 tablespoon (8 g) of the spice mixture to another bowl and set it aside to season the potatoes. Rub both pieces of the tenderloin with the remaining seasoning mixture. Set aside.

Preheat the air fryer to 350°F (180°C). Spray the air fryer basket with oil. Place both pieces of tenderloin in the air fryer basket and spray lightly with oil. Cook the tenderloin for approximately 20 minutes, turning halfway through, until a thermometer inserted in the center of the tenderloin reads 145°F (63°C). While the tenderloin cooks, place the potatoes in a medium bowl. Add the reserved tablespoon (8 g) of seasoning mixture and the olive oil. Toss gently to coat the potatoes.

Transfer the tenderloin pieces to a platter and tent with foil to rest for 10 minutes. While the tenderloin rests, place the potatoes in the air fryer. Increase the air fryer temperature to 400°F (200°C) and cook the potatoes for 8 to 10 minutes, tossing once halfway through cooking, until golden brown. Serve immediately alongside the pork tenderloin.

Sonoran Hot Dogs

The Sonoran hot dog originated in the Mexican state of Sonora in the 1980s and is now sold by street cart vendors known as "dogueros" throughout the southwestern United States, particularly in Arizona. I tried as many versions of the Sonoran hot dog as I could on a family trip to Tucson, where nearly every street corner has a taco truck offering the city's unofficial signature dish. Each one was more delicious than the last.

In a Sonoran hot dog, the dog itself is wrapped in bacon—so already you are off to a good start—and served on a toasted bun with beans, tomato, avocado, onion, and a drizzle of cool Mexican crema. Of course, grilling the bacon-wrapped dogs is the traditional way to prepare them, but it is not always convenient to fire up the grill. Happily, the air fryer turns out crisp bacon and plump hot dogs in just 10 minutes.

4 large hot dogs

4 slices bacon (not thick-cut)

2 tablespoons (28 g) unsalted butter, at room temperature

4 fresh bolillo rolls or good-quality hot dog buns

½ cup (120 g) refried beans, warmed

1 avocado, diced

1 Roma tomato, diced

½ small red onion, diced

¼ cup (60 ml) Mexican crema, thinned with 1 tablespoon (15 ml) milk

Fresh cilantro leaves, for garnish

Lime wedges, for garnish

Hot sauce, for serving

—
Makes 4 hot dogs

Wrap each hot dog with a slice of bacon and secure with toothpicks at each end. Place the hot dogs on a plate and refrigerate for 30 minutes to help the bacon adhere to the hot dogs. While the hot dogs chill, spread butter on the cut portion of each bun.

Preheat the air fryer to 350°F (180°C). Arrange the hot dogs in the air fryer basket and cook for 8 minutes. Open the air fryer and turn the hot dogs to ensure they are cooking evenly on all sides. Cook for an additional 2 minutes until the bacon is crisp and golden and the hot dog is plump.

Transfer the hot dogs to a plate and keep warm. Place the buttered buns in the air fryer and cook at 350°F (180°C) for 1 to 2 minutes, until the buns are warm and the butter is melted.

To assemble, spread 2 tablespoons (30 g) of refried beans into each bun. Add a bacon-wrapped hot dog. Top with diced avocado, tomato, onion, and a drizzle of Mexican crema. Garnish with cilantro leaves and serve with lime wedges and hot sauce.

Teriyaki-Glazed Baby Back Ribs

A rub of Chinese five-spice powder followed by a sweet and savory teriyaki glaze builds deep flavor in these juicy, sticky-sweet Asian-inspired ribs. The ribs are cooked at two different temperatures in the air fryer to replicate the tenderness and flavor achieved through traditional "low and slow" all-day grilling. This takes more time than many air fryer recipes but a small fraction of the time it would take to get the same results in the oven or the grill.

To recreate an old-fashioned backyard cookout, enjoy these ribs with Low Country Hush Puppies (page 55), or Fried Green Tomatoes (page 54).

1 teaspoon Chinese five-spice powder

½ teaspoon garlic powder

1 teaspoon kosher salt

1 teaspoon black pepper

2½ to 3 pounds (1 to 1⅓ kg) rack baby back ribs, cut into 4 pieces

¼ cup (60 ml) soy sauce, preferably low-sodium

1 tablespoon (9.5 g) brown sugar

1 tablespoon (15 ml) vegetable oil

½ tablespoon (4 g) grated fresh ginger

1 clove garlic, minced

3 teaspoons rice vinegar

1 teaspoon toasted sesame oil

—
Serves 4

Combine the Chinese five-spice powder, garlic powder, salt, and pepper in a small bowl and whisk to combine. Place each rib section on a large piece of foil and sprinkle all over with the spice mixture. Wrap the foil tightly around each rib section.

Arrange the foil-wrapped ribs in the air fryer basket. Set the temperature to 250°F (120°C) and cook for 50 minutes. While the ribs are cooking, combine the soy sauce, brown sugar, oil, ginger, garlic, rice vinegar, and sesame oil in a small bowl and whisk until combined.

After 50 minutes, use tongs to remove the ribs from the air fryer and place on a rimmed baking sheet. Allow the ribs to cool slightly, then carefully remove from the foil.

Brush the ribs evenly with the sauce mixture and return to the air fryer. Set the temperature to 400°F (200°C) and cook for 10 minutes, occasionally basting the ribs with additional sauce. The ribs should be crispy, tender, and slightly charred when cooked. Brush the cooked ribs with any remaining sauce and serve immediately.

Monte Cristo Sandwich

The Monte Cristo sandwich is an old-fashioned, classic diner-menu item. It is a combination of a grilled ham and cheese sandwich and French toast and is somewhat related to the classic French café sandwich, the croque monsieur. The diner version of a Monte Cristo is cooked in copious amounts of butter, which makes an already heavy dish even heavier. The air fryer version, however, needs just a spray of oil.

This recipe begs to be customized. You can make your Monte Cristo with just ham, just turkey, or a combination. Similarly, you can spread the bread with both mayonnaise and Dijon mustard, just mustard, or just mayonnaise. Lastly, there is the controversial dusting of powdered sugar: some people find it absolutely essential to a Monte Cristo, while others—okay, me—find this particular combination to be strange. I leave it to you to decide.

8 slices brioche or other soft, white bread

¼ cup (60 g) Dijon mustard

¼ cup (60 g) mayonnaise

½ pound (225 g) sliced deli ham, turkey, or a combination (about 12 slices total)

8 ounces (225 g) Swiss or Gruyère cheese, grated

2 eggs

2 tablespoons (30 ml) milk

1 cup (50 g) panko bread crumbs

Vegetable oil for spraying

Powdered sugar for dusting (optional)

—

Serves 4

Take 2 pieces of bread and spread 1 side with approximately ½ tablespoon (7 g) mustard and the other side with approximately ½ tablespoon (7 g) mayonnaise. Place 3 slices of ham, turkey, or a combination thereof on 1 piece of bread and top with approximately ½ cup (60 g) of the grated cheese. Top with the second slice of bread. Repeat with the remaining bread, deli meat, and cheese until you have assembled 4 sandwiches. Press down firmly on each sandwich with a metal spatula until the sandwiches are thin and compressed.

Beat the eggs with the milk in a shallow bowl. Spread the panko on a plate. Dip the pressed sandwiches in the egg mixture, shaking off any excess, then dredge both sides in the panko.

Spray the basket of the air fryer and both sides of 2 of the sandwiches with oil. Place 1 or 2 sandwiches in the air fryer, depending on the size, and cook at 400°F (200°C) for 8 to 10 minutes, flipping once halfway through, until both sides of the sandwich are browned and crispy and the cheese is melted. Repeat with the remaining sandwiches.

Serve the sandwiches warm with a dusting of powdered sugar, if desired.

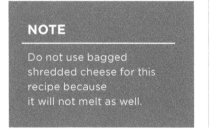

NOTE

Do not use bagged shredded cheese for this recipe because it will not melt as well.

Seafood

Confetti Salmon Burgers   112

Fried Shrimp with Sweet Chili Dipping Sauce   113

Teriyaki Salmon and Broccoli   114

Pecan-Crusted Tilapia   116

Maryland Crab Cakes with Sriracha Mayonnaise   117

Baja Fish Tacos   118

Jalea (Peruvian Fried Seafood with Salsa Criolla)   120

Bolivian Croquetas (Tuna-Stuffed Quinoa Patties)   122

Shrimp DeJonghe Skewers   123

Confetti Salmon Burgers

The key to this recipe is mincing the vegetables very finely. Cutting these firm vegetables into small pieces ensures that they will cook and become tender in the air fryer, eliminating the need to sauté them on the stove before mixing them into the salmon. The small pieces of colorful vegetables also give this recipe its name—they look just like pretty pieces of confetti.

Many recipes for salmon burgers call for mayonnaise as a binder, but some people do not care for mayonnaise or would prefer not to add extra calories to an otherwise healthy meal. I find that egg and bread crumbs are sufficient to hold the salmon burgers together, but I do recommend chilling the burgers prior to cooking to allow them to firm up. I like to serve these salmon burgers on a buttered brioche bun with lettuce.

14 ounces (400 g) cooked fresh or canned salmon, flaked with a fork

¼ cup (25 g) minced scallion, white and light green parts only

¼ cup (37.5 g) minced red bell pepper

¼ cup (30 g) minced celery

2 small lemons

1 teaspoon crab boil seasoning such as Old Bay

½ teaspoon kosher salt

½ teaspoon black pepper

1 egg, beaten

½ cup (25 g) fresh bread crumbs

Vegetable oil for spraying

—
Serves 4

In a large bowl, combine the salmon, vegetables, the zest and juice of 1 of the lemons, crab boil seasoning, salt, and pepper. Add the egg and bread crumbs and stir to combine. Form the mixture into 4 patties weighing approximately 5 ounces (140 g) each. Chill until firm, about 15 minutes.

Spray the salmon patties with oil on all sides and spray the air fryer basket to prevent sticking. Cook at 400°F (200°C) for 12 minutes, flipping halfway through, until the burgers are browned and cooked through. Cut the remaining lemon into 4 wedges and serve with the burgers.

Fried Shrimp with Sweet Chili Dipping Sauce

These golden-brown air-fried shrimp come out perfectly crisp just like their deep-fried counterparts without all the oil and mess. Adding mayonnaise to the egg wash creates a uniquely thick consistency that helps the panko bread crumbs stay on in the air fryer.

Snacking on these fried shrimp will transport you to summer days at your favorite beachfront clam shack. Reserve some of the sweet and spicy mayonnaise batter for a dipping sauce.

¾ cup (175 g) mayonnaise

1 tablespoon (15 ml) sriracha

2 tablespoons (30 ml) sweet chili sauce

1 teaspoon Worcestershire sauce

1 egg, beaten

1 cup (50 g) panko bread crumbs

1 pound (about 16; 455 g) raw shrimp, shelled and deveined

Vegetable oil for spraying

Lime wedges for serving

—
Makes 16 shrimp, to serve 4 as a first course

Combine the mayonnaise, sriracha, chili sauce, and Worcestershire sauce in a medium, shallow bowl and stir until smooth. Pour ⅓ cup (70 g) of the mixture into a separate bowl and reserve it to use as a dipping sauce.

Combine the beaten egg with the remaining mayonnaise mixture and stir until smooth. Place the panko in a shallow bowl. Pat the shrimp dry with paper towels. Dip the shrimp into the mayonnaise mixture, shaking off any excess, then dredge in the panko. Place the breaded shrimp on a plate or rack.

Preheat the air fryer to 360°F (182°C). Spray the basket of the air fryer lightly with oil. Arrange 8 shrimp in the basket and spray with additional oil. Cook the shrimp for 8 to 10 minutes, turning once halfway through, until the shrimp are golden brown. Remove from the air fryer and repeat with the remaining shrimp. Serve the shrimp immediately with the reserved sauce and lime wedges.

Teriyaki Salmon and Broccoli

This is the air fryer equivalent of a sheet pan dinner. Cook the salmon and broccoli together in the air fryer for a healthy, ready-all-at-once meal. Round it out with some jasmine rice if you are so inclined. If you are serving more than two, simply double the recipe and cook it in two batches. Or make two batches and use the leftover salmon to make Confetti Salmon Burgers (page 112) later in the week.

If you can find it, try this recipe with wild-caught salmon, which has richer flavor and a deeper hue than farm-raised. Wild-caught salmon, which is in season from May through September, is leaner than farm-raised, so be sure not to overcook it. The air fryer does a better job than the oven of keeping salmon from drying out.

¼ cup (60 ml) soy sauce, divided

2 tablespoons (30 ml) rice vinegar

1 tablespoon (15 g) brown sugar

¼ teaspoon grated fresh ginger

¼ cup (60 ml) plus 1 tablespoon (15 ml) vegetable oil

2 skin-on salmon fillets (6 ounces or 170 g each), at least 1 inch (2.5 cm) thick

6 cups (approximately 1 pound [455 g]) broccoli florets

Pinch red pepper flakes

Kosher salt and pepper to taste

—

Serves 2

To make the teriyaki marinade, whisk together 2 tablespoons (30 ml) of the soy sauce, the rice vinegar, brown sugar, and ginger in a small bowl until the sugar is dissolved. Slowly pour in the ¼ cup (60 ml) of oil in a steady stream while whisking. Place the salmon fillets in a small glass baking dish and cover with the marinade. Cover and refrigerate for at least 15 minutes but no more than a half hour.

Meanwhile, toss the broccoli florets with the remaining soy sauce and oil and red pepper flakes. Season with salt and pepper. Place the broccoli florets in a single layer in the basket of the air fryer. Place the salmon fillets on top of or nestled alongside the broccoli, skin side down. Cook at 375°F (190°C) for 8 to 10 minutes until the broccoli is tender and charred and the salmon flakes easily with a fork. (Wild-caught salmon should be cooked to an internal temperature of 120°F [49°C].) Serve immediately.

Pecan-Crusted Tilapia

Ground pecans add a different texture and a pleasant nuttiness to the breading on these tilapia fillets while the Cajun spices in the coating give them just the right amount of zing. With its mild flavor and flaky texture, tilapia can convert even those who claim not to like fish. Picky eaters are no match for these flaky, crunchy fillets that cook up in just 10 minutes in the air fryer.

While a simple squeeze of lemon is enough to make these fillets sing, for a special treat that doubles down on the Cajun flavor, serve them with homemade Rémoulade (page 54).

1¼ cups (125 g) pecans

¾ cup (39 g) panko bread crumbs

½ cup (63 g) all-purpose flour

2 tablespoons (18 g) Cajun seasoning

2 eggs beaten with 2 tablespoons (30 ml) water

4 tilapia fillets (6 to 8 ounces, or 170 to 225 g each)

Vegetable oil for spraying

Lemons for serving

—
Serves 4

Grind the pecans in the food processor until they resemble coarse meal. Combine the ground pecans with the panko on a plate. On a second plate, combine the flour and Cajun seasoning. Dry the tilapia fillets using paper towels and dredge them in the flour mixture, shaking off any excess. Dip the fillets in the egg mixture and then dredge them in the pecan and panko mixture, pressing the coating onto the fillets. Place the breaded fillets on a plate or rack.

Preheat the air fryer to 375°F (190°C). Spray both sides of the breaded fillets with oil. Carefully transfer 2 of the fillets to the air fryer basket and cook for 9 to 10 minutes, flipping once halfway through, until the flesh is opaque and flaky. Repeat with the remaining fillets.

Serve immediately with lemon wedges.

Maryland Crab Cakes with Sriracha Mayonnaise

I grew up near Maryland where crab cakes seasoned with Old Bay are a local delicacy. I have always enjoyed them in restaurants but have not had much success cooking them at home because the cakes always seem to fall apart in the frying pan. The air fryer, however, turns out moist, flavorful crab cakes with less mess—no splattering oil!—and less fat. Chilling the crab cakes before baking will help them hold together as they cook in the air fryer.

These crab cakes get an extra kick from sriracha, a chile-based condiment popular in Thai cuisine and available in the Asian foods section of most supermarkets. Serve with a sriracha mayonnaise dipping sauce on the side.

SRIRACHA MAYONNAISE

1 cup (225 g) mayonnaise

1 tablespoon (15 ml) sriracha

1½ teaspoons (8 ml) freshly squeezed lemon juice

CRAB CAKES

1 teaspoon extra-virgin olive oil

¼ cup (37.5 g) finely diced red bell pepper

¼ cup (40 g) diced onion

¼ cup (30 g) diced celery

1 pound (455 g) lump crabmeat

1 teaspoon Old Bay seasoning

1 egg

1½ teaspoons (8 ml) freshly squeezed lemon juice

1¾ cups (89 g) panko bread crumbs, divided

Vegetable oil for spraying

—

Makes 8 crab cakes, to serve 4

Mix the mayonnaise, sriracha, and lemon juice in a small bowl. Place ⅔ cup (150 g) of the mixture in a separate bowl to form the base of the crab cakes. Cover the remaining sriracha mayonnaise and refrigerate. (This will become dipping sauce for the crab cakes once they are cooked.)

Heat the olive oil in a heavy-bottomed, medium skillet over medium-high heat. Add the bell pepper, onion, and celery and sauté for 3 minutes. Transfer the vegetables to the bowl with the reserved ⅔ cup of sriracha mayonnaise. Mix in the crab, Old Bay seasoning, egg, and lemon juice. Add 1 cup (50 g) of the panko. Form the crab mixture into 8 cakes. Dredge the cakes in the remaining ¾ cup (39 g) of panko, turning to coat. Place on a baking sheet. Cover and refrigerate for at least 1 hour and up to 8 hours.

To cook, preheat the air fryer to 375°F (190°C). Spray the air fryer basket with oil. Working in batches as needed so as not to overcrowd the basket, place the chilled crab cakes in a single layer in the basket. Spray the crab cakes with oil. Cook until golden brown, 8 to 10 minutes, carefully turning halfway through cooking. Remove to a platter and keep warm. Repeat with the remaining crab cakes as needed. Serve the crab cakes immediately with sriracha mayonnaise dipping sauce.

Baja Fish Tacos

Fish tacos originated on the Baja Peninsula of Mexico sometime in the last century but have since spread all over North America. The basic version—and arguably the best—consists of nothing more than battered and fried white fish wrapped in a corn tortilla—or two for more stability—topped with a few shreds of cabbage, some pico de gallo, a dollop of creamy sauce, and an essential spritz of lime.

This version hews pretty close to the classic recipe with the primary difference being that these fillets are air fried, not deep-fried, but they are no less delectably crispy. The secret is the mayonnaise-based batter, which keeps the fish tender and moist. Use freshly made pico de gallo or a tropical fruit-based salsa to top your tacos. Elotes (page 56) would make an excellent accompaniment.

FRIED FISH

1 pound (455 g) tilapia fillets (or other mild white fish)

½ cup (63 g) all-purpose flour

1 teaspoon garlic powder

1 teaspoon kosher salt

¼ teaspoon cayenne pepper

½ cup (115 g) mayonnaise

3 tablespoons (45 ml) milk

1¾ cups (89 g) panko bread crumbs

Vegetable oil for spraying

TACOS

8 corn tortillas

¼ head red or green cabbage, shredded

1 ripe avocado, halved and each half cut into 4 slices

12 ounces (340 g) pico de gallo or other fresh salsa

Mexican crema

1 lime, cut into wedges

—
Makes 8 tacos, to serve 4

To make the fish, cut the fish fillets into strips 3 to 4 inches (7.5 to 10 cm) long and 1 inch (2.5 cm) wide. Combine the flour, garlic powder, salt, and cayenne pepper on a plate and whisk to combine. In a shallow bowl, whisk the mayonnaise and milk together. Place the panko on a separate plate. Dredge the fish strips in the seasoned flour, shaking off any excess. Dip the strips in the mayonnaise mixture, coating them completely, then dredge in the panko, shaking off any excess. Place the fish strips on a plate or rack.

Working in batches, spray half the fish strips with oil and arrange them in the basket of the air fryer, taking care not to crowd them. Cook at 400°F (200°C) for 4 minutes, then flip and cook for another 3 to 4 minutes until the outside is brown and crisp and the inside is opaque and flakes easily with a fork. Repeat with the remaining strips.

Heat the tortillas in the microwave or on the stovetop. To assemble the tacos, place 2 fish strips inside each tortilla. Top with shredded cabbage, a slice of avocado, pico de gallo, and a dollop of crema. Serve with a lime wedge on the side.

Jalea (Peruvian Fried Seafood with Salsa Criolla)

Many countries—at least island nations or those with long coastlines—have a tradition of fried seafood, from England's fish and chips to Italy's fritto misto. In Peru, there is jalea, a heaping platter of fried fish and shellfish topped with *salsa criollo*, a piquant salad of onion, tomato, and cilantro swimming in lime juice. When served at a Lima ceviche restaurant, jalea is battered and deep-fried, but our homemade version is coated in crispy bread crumbs and air fried with just a spritz of oil. With the vegetable salad served right on top of the fried seafood, jalea is a complete one-dish meal.

SALSA CRIOLLA

½ red onion, thinly sliced

2 tomatoes, diced

1 serrano or jalapeño pepper, seeded and diced

1 clove garlic, minced

¼ cup (4 g) chopped fresh cilantro

Pinch kosher salt

3 limes

FRIED SEAFOOD

1 pound (455 g) firm, white-fleshed fish such as cod (add an extra ½ pound [225 g] fish if not using shrimp)

20 large or jumbo shrimp, shelled and deveined

¼ cup (31 g) all-purpose flour

¼ cup (32 g) cornstarch

1 teaspoon garlic powder

1 teaspoon kosher salt

¼ teaspoon cayenne pepper

2 cups (100 g) panko bread crumbs

2 eggs, beaten with 2 tablespoons (30 ml) water

Vegetable oil for spraying

Mayonnaise or tartar sauce for serving (optional)

—

Serves 4

To make the Salsa Criolla, combine the red onion, tomatoes, pepper, garlic, cilantro, and salt in a medium bowl. Add the juice and zest of 2 of the limes. Refrigerate the salad while you cook the fish.

To make the seafood, cut the fish fillets into strips approximately 2 inches (5 cm) long and 1 inch (2.5 cm) wide. Place the flour, cornstarch, garlic powder, salt, and cayenne pepper on a plate and whisk to combine. Place the panko on a separate plate. Dredge the fish strips in the seasoned flour mixture, shaking off any excess. Dip the strips in the egg mixture, coating them completely, then dredge in the panko, shaking off any excess. Place the fish strips on a plate or rack. Repeat with the shrimp, if using.

Spray the basket of the air fryer with oil. Working in 2 or 3 batches, arrange the fish and shrimp in a single layer in the basket of the air fryer, taking care not to crowd the basket. Spray with oil. Cook at 400°F (200°C) for 5 minutes, then flip and cook for another 4 to 5 minutes until the outside is brown and crisp and the inside of the fish is opaque and flakes easily with a fork. Repeat with the remaining seafood.

Place the fried seafood on a platter. Use a slotted spoon to remove the salsa criolla from the bowl, leaving behind any liquid that has accumulated. Place the salsa criolla on top of the fried seafood. Serve immediately with the remaining lime, cut into wedges, and mayonnaise or tartar sauce as desired.

Bolivian Croquetas (Tuna-Stuffed Quinoa Patties)

Quinoa, an ancient grain from South America, has become trendy of late because it is gluten free, high in protein, and has a sweet, nutty flavor. Just as many cuisines have croquettes made with leftover rice or potatoes, in Andean cuisine, quinoa forms the base for a *croqueta* filled with ham and cheese or, as here, tuna. These tuna-stuffed quinoa patties are packed with protein and require only basic pantry ingredients, so you can whip up a quick and healthy meal even when it feels like there is no food in the house.

Although quinoa itself is gluten free, this recipe calls for bread and panko bread crumbs, both of which contain gluten. However, these patties can easily be made without any gluten, if that is important to you, by substituting gluten-free sandwich bread and gluten-free panko bread crumbs, which are readily available.

12 ounces (340 g) quinoa

4 slices white bread with crusts removed

½ cup (120 ml) milk

3 eggs

10 ounces (280 g) tuna packed in olive oil, drained

2 to 3 lemons

Kosher salt and pepper to taste

1¼ cups (63 g) panko bread crumbs

Vegetable oil for spraying

Lemon wedges for serving

—
Makes 12 croquettes, to serve 4

Rinse the quinoa in a fine-mesh sieve until the water runs clear. Bring 4 cups (960 ml) of salted water to a boil. Add the quinoa, cover, and reduce heat to low. Simmer the quinoa covered until most of the water is absorbed and the quinoa is tender, 15 to 20 minutes. Drain and allow to cool to room temperature. Meanwhile, soak the bread in the milk.

Mix the drained quinoa with the soaked bread and 2 of the eggs in a large bowl and mix thoroughly. In a medium bowl, combine the tuna, the remaining egg, and the juice and zest of 1 of the lemons. Season well with salt and pepper. Spread the panko on a plate.

Scoop up approximately ½ cup (82.5 g) of the quinoa mixture and flatten into a patty. Place a heaping tablespoon (14 g) of the tuna mixture in the center of the patty and close the quinoa around the tuna. Flatten the patty slightly to create an oval-shaped croquette. Dredge both sides of the croquette in the panko. Repeat with the remaining quinoa and tuna.

Spray the basket of the air fryer with oil to prevent sticking. Arrange 4 or 5 of the croquettes in the basket of the air fryer, taking care to avoid overcrowding. Spray the tops of the croquettes with oil. Cook at 400°F (200°C) for 8 minutes until the top side is browned and crispy. Carefully turn the croquettes over and spray the second side with oil. Cook until the second side is browned and crispy, another 7 minutes. Repeat with the remaining croquettes.

Serve the croquetas warm with plenty of lemon wedges for spritzing.

Shrimp DeJonghe Skewers

Shrimp DeJonghe originated in the late nineteenth or early twentieth century at DeJonghe's Hotel and Restaurant in Chicago and has been a staple on Chicago steakhouse menus ever since. Traditionally prepared by baking whole, peeled shrimp in a mixture of garlic-laced bread crumbs, butter, and sherry, the dish can be served as a decadent appetizer or as a main dish over pasta.

The mixture of butter and bread crumbs lends itself especially well to the air fryer. Lacing the shrimp on skewers before coating them with butter and bread crumbs creates a lighter and crispier take on the original. These make a special main dish when served alongside rice or pasta and a green salad.

2 teaspoons sherry

3 tablespoons (42 g) unsalted butter, melted

1 cup (50 g) panko bread crumbs

3 cloves garlic, minced

⅓ cup (20 g) minced flat-leaf parsley plus more for garnish

1 teaspoon kosher salt

Pinch cayenne pepper

1½ pounds (680 g) shrimp, peeled and deveined

Vegetable oil for spraying

Lemon wedges for serving

—

Makes 8 skewers, to serve 4

Stir the sherry and melted butter together in a shallow bowl or pie plate and whisk until combined. Set aside. Whisk together the panko, garlic, parsley, salt, and cayenne pepper on a large plate or shallow bowl.

Thread the shrimp onto metal skewers designed for the air fryer or bamboo skewers, 3 to 4 per skewer. Dip 1 shrimp skewer in the butter mixture, then dredge in the panko mixture until each shrimp is lightly coated. Place the skewer on a plate or rimmed baking sheet and repeat the process with the remaining skewers.

Preheat the air fryer to 350°F (180°C). Arrange 4 skewers in the air fryer basket. Spray the skewers with oil and cook for 8 minutes, until the bread crumbs are golden brown and the shrimp are cooked through. Transfer the cooked skewers to a serving plate and keep warm while cooking the remaining 4 skewers in the air fryer.

Sprinkle the cooked skewers with additional fresh parsley and serve with lemon wedges if desired.

NOTE

If using bamboo skewers, soak them in water for 30 minutes to prevent burning. Six-inch (15 cm) skewers fit easily in the air fryer basket. If using longer skewers, simply break off the end to ensure the skewers will fit in the basket.

CHAPTER 5
Desserts

Churros with Chocolate Dipping Sauce   126

Lemon-Lavender Doughnuts   128

Chouquettes (French Pastry Puffs)   131

Profiteroles   132

Chocolate Chip Pan Cookie Sundae   134

Caramelized Peach Shortcakes   136

Caramelized Pineapple with Mint and Lime   138

Churros with Chocolate Dipping Sauce

Churros are another deep-fried treat that few people attempt to make at home—for all the usual reasons. But with the air fryer, it is easy to make homemade churros with only a few modifications to the traditional recipe and a fraction of the fat.

When you buy churros on the street in Spain or Latin America, they are often long and sometimes even curved into a large teardrop. To fit the air fryer, these churros are shorter—more like churro bites. But don't change one important tradition: serve these cinnamon-dusted churros with a chocolate dipping sauce for a very special dessert.

CHOCOLATE SAUCE

4 ounces (115 g) semisweet chocolate, finely chopped

½ cup (120 ml) heavy cream

¼ cup (85 g) light corn syrup

½ teaspoon cinnamon

¼ teaspoon cayenne pepper

CHURROS

3 tablespoons (45 g) unsalted butter, divided

1 cup (240 ml) water

½ cup (100 g) granulated sugar plus 1 tablespoon (13 g)

Pinch kosher salt

1 cup (125 g) all-purpose flour

2 eggs

Vegetable oil for spraying

2 teaspoons cinnamon

—
Makes 12 to 14 churros, to serve 4

To make the chocolate sauce, place the chopped chocolate in a heat-proof bowl. Combine the cream and corn syrup in a small saucepan and bring to a simmer. Pour the warm cream mixture over the chocolate and stir until the chocolate is melted. Add the cinnamon and cayenne pepper. Set aside.

To make the churros, combine 1 tablespoon (14 g) of the butter, the water, 1 tablespoon (13 g) of the sugar, and the salt in a medium saucepan. Melt the butter over low heat. Add the flour and stir vigorously to form a dough ball. Continue to cook, stirring until the mixture looks dry and thick, 2 minutes. Remove from the heat and allow to cool to room temperature. Once cool, beat in the eggs one at a time, making sure the first egg is fully incorporated before adding the second. Continue beating until the mixture is smooth. Let the dough rest for 30 minutes.

Place the churros batter into a piping bag outfitted with an extra-large tip, round or star-shaped. Spray the basket of the air fryer with oil. Working in batches, pipe churros that are 5 to 6 inches (13 to 15 cm) long and ¾ to 1 inch (2 to 2.5 cm) in diameter directly onto the air fryer basket. Do not crowd the basket. Use a knife or scissors to cut the dough when you've reached the desired length. Spray the churros with oil.

Cook at 360°F (182°C) for 12 to 14 minutes until the outside is firm and brown and the inside is soft. While the churros are cooking, combine the remaining ½ cup (100 g) sugar with the cinnamon on a plate and whisk to combine. Melt the remaining 2 tablespoons (30 g) of butter and place in a small dish.

Remove the cooked churros from the air fryer and immediately brush with melted butter and dredge in the cinnamon sugar. Repeat the process with the remaining churros. Serve hot with the chocolate sauce.

Lemon-Lavender Doughnuts

This recipe makes a classic American-style yeast-risen doughnut, but without the hassle and mess of deep-frying. Lemon zest in the batter and lemon juice in the glaze combine to create a doughnut with a bright, sweet-tart, citrus flavor. Because lemon and lavender is one of my favorite combinations, I sprinkle just a few buds of lavender on top of the glazed doughnuts. If lemon is not your thing, you can omit it entirely and use milk and vanilla extract for the glaze.

An overnight rise is traditional for doughnuts, and I think it breaks up the work into more manageable parts. The overnight rise is especially convenient if you are planning to serve the doughnuts in the morning.

½ cup (120 ml) milk, warmed to between 100°F and 110°F (38°C to 43°C)

1 teaspoon yeast

¼ cup (50 g) granulated sugar, divided

2 cups (250 g) all-purpose flour

½ teaspoon kosher salt

Zest and juice of 1 lemon

4 tablespoons (55 g) unsalted butter, melted

1 egg

Vegetable oil for spraying

1½ cups (150 g) powdered sugar, sifted

Dried lavender for culinary use (optional)

—
Makes 6 to 8 doughnuts

Combine the warm milk, yeast, and a pinch of the sugar in a small bowl and whisk to combine. Allow to sit until the yeast blooms and looks bubbly, about 5 to 10 minutes. Meanwhile, whisk together the remaining sugar, flour, and salt. Add the zest of the lemon to the dry ingredients.

When the yeast has bloomed, add the milk mixture to the dry ingredients and stir to combine. Add the melted butter and the egg and stir to form a thick dough. Turn the dough out onto a well-floured board and knead until smooth, 1 to 2 minutes. Place the dough in an oiled bowl, cover, and allow to rise in the refrigerator overnight.

The following day, remove the dough from the refrigerator and allow it to come to room temperature. Turn the risen dough out onto a well-floured board. Roll the dough out until it is approximately ¼ inch (6 mm) thick. Using a 3- or 4-inch (7.5 or 10 cm) circular cookie cutter, cut out as many doughnuts as possible. Use a 1-inch (2.5 cm) round cookie cutter to cut out holes from the center of each doughnut. With the dough scraps, you can either cut out additional doughnut holes using the 1-inch (2.5 cm) cutter or, if desired, gather the scraps and roll them out again to cut out more doughnuts. (The doughnuts from the rerolled scraps will not rise as well as the other doughnuts.)

Transfer the doughnuts and doughnut holes to a lined baking sheet. Cover with a clean kitchen towel and allow to proof in a warm place until puffy and, when pressed with a finger, the dough slowly springs back, 30 minutes to 1 hour.

(continued)

(continued)

While the dough is proofing, prepare the glaze. In a medium bowl, whisk together the sifted powdered sugar and the juice from the lemon. Set aside.

When the doughnuts have proofed, spray the basket of the air fryer with oil. Transfer no more than 3 or 4 of the doughnuts and 2 or 3 of the holes to the air fryer basket. Spray the doughnuts lightly with oil. Cook at 360°F (182°C) for 5 to 6 minutes, flipping once halfway through, until browned and cooked through. Transfer the cooked doughnuts and holes to a cooling rack and repeat with the remaining doughnuts and holes.

Once the doughnuts are cool enough to handle, dip the tops into the glaze. Return the dipped doughnuts to the rack to allow the excess glaze to drip off. Once the glaze has hardened, dip each doughnut again to create a nice opaque finish. While the second glaze is still wet, if desired, sprinkle a few buds of lavender on top of each doughnut.

Chouquettes (French Pastry Puffs)

The closest thing that traditional French baking has to a doughnut is a chouquette, a small puff of choux pastry topped with crunchy pearl sugar. French *patisseries* sell them by the bagful as an afternoon snack to hungry schoolchildren. Paris-based pastry chef and author David Lebovitz is credited with introducing chouquettes to an American audience.

Chouquettes are surprisingly easy to make and take less than 20 minutes to bake in the air fryer. The only tricky part will likely be finding pearl sugar, which is sometimes called Swedish pearl sugar. (It's so Swedish, in fact, that Ikea sells it.) These white, irregularly shaped chunks of sugar do not melt or burn when sprinkled on top of pastries or breads prior to baking and add a satisfying crunch. You can order pearl sugar online.

3 tablespoons (45 g) unsalted butter

1 tablespoon (13 g) granulated sugar

1 cup (240 ml) water

1 cup (125 g) all-purpose flour

3 eggs

1½ tablespoons (25 ml) milk

Vegetable oil for brushing

½ cup (96 g) pearl sugar

—
Makes 20 chouquettes, to serve 4 or 5

Combine the butter, granulated sugar, and water in a medium saucepan and melt the butter over low heat. Add the flour and stir to form a cohesive dough. Cook over medium-low heat for 2 minutes to get rid of the raw flour taste. Remove from the heat and allow to cool to room temperature. Beat in 2 of the eggs, one at a time, making sure the first egg is fully incorporated before the adding the second. The dough will look curdled at first, but keep beating vigorously until the dough becomes smooth. Once the eggs are fully incorporated, let the dough rest for 30 minutes.

Beat the remaining egg together with the milk in a small bowl. Lightly brush the basket of the air fryer with oil. Using a small, spring-loaded cookie scoop or a tablespoon, scoop 6 to 8 circles of dough directly onto the basket of the air fryer. Brush the tops of the dough with the egg wash and generously sprinkle on pearl sugar. (Try to crowd the tops with as much pearl sugar as possible because the dough will expand when baked.)

Cook at 360°F (182°C) for 15 to 17 minutes until the outside of the chouquettes is golden brown and the inside fully cooked and airy. Repeat 2 more times with the remaining dough. Serve immediately.

Profiteroles

A staple of French bistro dessert menus, profiteroles are composed of choux buns—the same kind used for cream puffs—filled with ice cream and topped with a rich chocolate sauce.

These easy air fryer profiteroles are such a fun way to end a dinner party. They look elegant but are nothing more than a dressed-up ice cream sundae, and who ever said no to an ice cream sundae? For easier serving, scoop the ice cream into balls in advance and place the balls in a small metal baking pan. Cover the pan and freeze until needed. Then, when dinner is over, you can easily assemble the profiteroles.

CHOUX PUFFS

3 tablespoons (45 g) unsalted butter

1 tablespoon (13 g) granulated sugar

1 cup (235 ml) water

1 cup (125 g) all-purpose flour

2 eggs

Vegetable oil for brushing

CHOCOLATE SAUCE

4 ounces (115 g) semisweet chocolate, finely chopped

2 tablespoons (28 g) unsalted butter at room temperature

1 cup (240 ml) heavy cream

¼ cup (85 g) corn syrup

1 pint (285 g) vanilla ice cream for serving

—
Makes 8 to 10 profiteroles, to serve 4 or 5

Combine the butter, sugar, and water in a medium saucepan and melt the butter over low heat. Add the flour and stir to form a cohesive dough. Cook over medium-low heat for 2 minutes to get rid of the raw flour taste. Remove from the heat and allow to cool to room temperature. Beat the eggs in one at a time, making sure the first egg is fully incorporated before the adding the second. The dough will look curdled at first, but keep beating vigorously until the dough becomes smooth. Once the eggs are fully incorporated, let the dough rest for 30 minutes.

While the dough is resting, make the chocolate sauce. Place the chopped chocolate and butter in a heat-proof bowl. Heat the cream and corn syrup in a small saucepan over medium heat until the cream is simmering. Remove from the heat and pour the cream mixture over the chocolate in the bowl. Stir until the chocolate and butter have melted and the sauce is smooth. Set aside.

Once the dough has rested, place it in a piping bag outfitted with a large, round tip. Lightly oil the basket of the air fryer. Working in 2 batches, pipe round puffs of dough approximately 2 inches (5 cm) wide and 1 inch (2.5 cm) tall directly onto the basket of the air fryer. Use a knife or scissors to cut the dough when you have achieved the desired size. With a damp finger, press down on the swirl at the top of each puff to round it. Cook at 360°F (182°C) for 18 to 20 minutes until the outside of the puffs is golden brown and crisp and the inside is fully cooked and airy.

To serve, halve the choux puffs crosswise and place a scoop of ice cream inside each one. Replace the top of the puff and spoon chocolate sauce over the top. Serve immediately.

Chocolate Chip Pan Cookie Sundae

My favorite thing about this chocolate chip pan cookie is how quickly it comes together—and with just one bowl! You can decide to make it on the spur of the moment—right before sitting down to dinner, for example—and 25 minutes later, your family will be digging into a warm, gooey pan cookie topped with vanilla ice cream and hot fudge. What a special way to keep everyone at the table a little longer. This is an easy, forgiving recipe that kids and teens can make by themselves when they have friends over.

1 stick (4 ounces, or 112 g) unsalted butter, softened

3 tablespoons (39 g) granulated sugar

3 tablespoons (28.5 g) brown sugar

1 egg

1 teaspoon vanilla extract

½ cup (63 g) all-purpose flour

¼ teaspoon baking soda

¼ teaspoon kosher salt

½ cup (88 g) semisweet chocolate chips

Vegetable oil for spraying

Vanilla ice cream for serving

Hot fudge or caramel sauce for serving

—
Serves 4

In a medium bowl, cream the butter and sugars together using a handheld mixer until light and fluffy. Add the egg and vanilla and mix until combined. In a small bowl, whisk together the flour, baking soda, and salt. Add the dry ingredients to the batter and mix until combined. Add the chocolate chips and mix a final time.

Preheat the air fryer to 325°F (170°C). Lightly grease a 7-inch (18 cm) pizza pan insert for the air fryer. Spread the batter evenly in the pan. Place the pan in the air fryer and cook for 12 to 15 minutes, until the top of the cookie is browned and the middle is gooey but cooked. Remove the pan from the air fryer.

Place 1 to 2 scoops of vanilla ice cream in the center of the cookie and top with hot fudge or caramel sauce, as you prefer. Pass around spoons and eat the cookie sundae right out of the pan.

Caramelized Peach Shortcakes

If strawberry shortcake knew about caramelized peach shortcake, it would retire. Luscious summer peaches with just a hint of caramelization are the perfect foil for a not-too-sweet biscuit and some whipped cream. You can also try this same method of caramelizing fruit in the air fryer with other stone fruits, such as nectarines and apricots—whatever looks good at the farmers market!

For convenience, you can make the biscuits and the whipped cream in advance. The peaches are best served warm.

SHORTCAKES

1 cup (125 g) self-rising flour

½ cup (120 ml) plus 1 tablespoon (15 ml) heavy cream

Vegetable oil for spraying

CARAMELIZED PEACHES

2 peaches, preferably freestone

1 tablespoon (14 g) unsalted butter, melted

2 teaspoons brown sugar

1 teaspoon cinnamon

WHIPPED CREAM

1 cup (240 ml) cold heavy cream

1 tablespoon (13 g) granulated sugar

½ teaspoon vanilla extract

Zest of 1 lime

—
Serves 4

To make the shortcakes, place the flour in a medium bowl and whisk to remove any lumps. Make a well in the center of the flour. While stirring with a fork, slowly pour in ½ cup (120 ml) plus 1 tablespoon (15 ml) of the heavy cream. Continue to stir until the dough has mostly come together. With your hands, gather the dough, incorporating any dry flour, and form into a ball.

Place the dough on a lightly floured board and pat into a rectangle that is ½ to ¾ inch (1.3 to 2 cm) thick. Fold in half. Turn and repeat. Pat the dough into a ¾-inch-thick (2 cm) square. Cut dough into 4 equally sized square biscuits.

Preheat the air fryer to 325°F (170°C). Spray the air fryer basket with oil to prevent sticking. Place the biscuits in the air fryer basket. Cook for 15 to 18 minutes until the tops are browned and the insides fully cooked. (May be done ahead.)

To make the peaches, cut the peaches in half and remove the pit. Brush the peach halves with the melted butter and sprinkle ½ teaspoon of the brown sugar and ¼ teaspoon of the cinnamon on each peach half. Arrange the peaches in a single layer in the air fryer basket. Cook at 375°F (190°C) for 8 to 10 minutes until the peaches are soft and the tops caramelized.

While the peaches are cooking, whip the cream. Pour the cold heavy cream, sugar, and vanilla (if using) into the bowl of a stand mixer or a metal mixing bowl. Beat with the whisk attachment for your stand mixer or a handheld electric mixer on high speed until stiff peaks form, about 1 minute. (If not using the cream right away, cover with plastic wrap and refrigerate until needed.)

To assemble the shortcakes, cut each biscuit in half horizontally. Place a peach on the bottom half of each biscuit and place the top half on top of the peach. Top each shortcake with whipped cream and a sprinkle of lime zest. Serve immediately.

Caramelized Pineapple with Mint and Lime

Raw pineapple is fine, especially if you happen to be enjoying some on a Hawaiian beach. But for me, pineapple realizes its full potential when it is grilled or roasted so that it softens and the fruit's natural sugars are concentrated. The air fryer makes it simple to caramelize pineapple with just a light kiss of butter and a sprinkle of brown sugar.

Cutting the pineapple into rings before caramelizing it makes this extremely simple, tropical-inspired dish pretty enough for a party. Enjoy air-fried pineapple on its own as a light summer dessert or, if you are feeling more indulgent, add a scoop of vanilla ice cream or coconut whipped cream.

1 pineapple

4 tablespoons (55 g) unsalted butter, melted

2 tablespoons (30 g) plus 2 teaspoons brown sugar

2 tablespoons (12 g) fresh mint, cut into ribbons

1 lime

—
Serves 4

Cut off the top and bottom of the pineapple and stand it on a cut end. Slice off the outer skin, cutting deeply enough to remove the eyes of the pineapple. Cut off any pointy edges to make the pineapple nice and round. Cut the peeled pineapple into 8 circles, approximately ½ to ¾ inch (1.3 to 2 cm) thick. Remove the core of each slice using a small, circular cookie or biscuit cutter, or simply cut out the core using a paring knife. Place the pineapple rings on a plate.

Brush both sides of the pineapple rings with the melted butter. Working in 2 batches, arrange 4 slices in a single layer in the basket of the air fryer. Sprinkle ½ teaspoon brown sugar on the top of each ring. Cook at 400°F (200°C) until the top side is browned and caramelized, about 10 minutes. With tongs, carefully flip each ring and sprinkle brown sugar on the second side. Cook for an additional 5 minutes until the second side is browned and caramelized. Remove the cooked pineapple and repeat with the remaining pineapple rings.

Arrange all the cooked pineapple rings on a serving plate or platter. Sprinkle with mint and spritz with the juice of the lime. Serve warm.

About the Author

Emily Paster travels the world in search of extraordinary food. Emily has sampled fry jacks from a roadside shack in Belize, Chinese soup dumplings along Vancouver's dumpling trail, beef heart anticuchos on a Peruvian horse ranch, trout poached in beeswax at a Michelin-starred restaurant in Vienna, and reindeer with cloudberries in a food hall in Stockholm. At home in Chicago, Emily's culinary and DIY adventures are inspired by the city's diverse neighborhoods, its global food markets, and the bounty of Midwestern farms—whether she is feeding her family of four, hosting a Yom Kippur breakfast for twenty, or developing a new recipe for an assignment.

Emily's recipes and writing have appeared in such print and online outlets as *O, The Oprah Magazine*, *Midwest Living*, *Allrecipes*, *Plate*, Food52, and more. She is the writer and photographer behind the website West of the Loop, which has been called "a family food blog to savor." Her previous books include *Food Swap: Specialty Recipes for Bartering, Sharing, and Giving* (2016) and *The Joys of Jewish Preserving* (2017), and *Epic Air Fryer.*

Acknowledgments

Writing these pages and developing the recipes was an intense and, for a brief period of time, an all-consuming process. But as much work as it was, I really enjoyed writing this book, and I am grateful to have had the opportunity to do so. For that, I thank my editor and friend Dan Rosenberg.

Thanks to the rest of the team at Quarto, including Anne Re, Jessi Schatz, and Todd Conly. Kathy Dvorsky provided thorough and professional copyediting, for which I am very grateful.

My fellow Oak Park–River Forest mom Rebecca Andexler—an extremely talented cook, recipe developer, and food stylist—stepped in to help with some of the recipes at a crucial juncture in the preparation of this manuscript and for that, I cannot thank her enough.

It was a pleasure to collaborate once again with the gifted Leigh Olson, who shot all of the mouthwatering photographs in this book. Enormous thanks to Leigh for taking on this project and for once again hosting me in her home studio. Thanks also to Leigh's husband, Eric Biermann, for his gracious hospitality.

Thanks to my friend Janice Moskoff, who cheered me on while I worked on this manuscript and even bought her husband an air fryer just so they could make the recipes in this book. (It helped that he had been wanting one for years.)

The wonderful staff at the River Forest Public Library quickly responded to my request to check out every single air fryer cookbook in the system. I am grateful to them, as always, for supporting my work and providing me with a quiet and peaceful place to write.

Thanks to the staff and teachers at the Oak Park School of Rock—especially Holly, Andy, Jack, Heidie, Rafe, Stephanie, and Michael—for being awesome musicians, inspiring role models, and very enthusiastic taste-testers.

Above all, a huge thank you to my husband, Elliot, and my children Zoe and Jamie Regenstein, who spent months eating almost exclusively air-fried food for dinner—and sometimes breakfast and lunch—and always gave me honest feedback.

Index

A

appetizers
Avocado Fries with Pomegranate
Molasses, 64
Caribbean Yuca Fries, 59
Chinese Takeout Egg Rolls with Soy-
Vinegar Dipping Sauce, 46
Chorizo Scotch Eggs, 37
Crab Rangoon, 48
Crispy Vegetable Spring Rolls, 44–45
Elotes (Mexican Street Corn), 56
Fried Green Tomatoes with
Rémoulade, 54
Fried Pickles with Buttermilk-Herb
Ranch Dressing, 42
KFC (Korean Fried Cauliflower), 66
Low Country Hush Puppies, 55
Orange and Rosemary Roasted
Chickpeas, 41
Pork and Cabbage Gyoza, 47
Potato and Cheese Taquitos, 36
Prosciutto-Wrapped Asparagus, 58
Roasted Garlic Guacamole with
Homemade Tortilla Chips, 50
Roasted Red Pepper and Feta Salad,
67
Smoky Eggplant Dip with
Homemade Pita Chips, 52
Spicy Maple-Soy Brussels Sprouts,
62
Supplì al Telefono (Roman Rice
Croquettes), 38–40
Tandoori Yogurt Dip with Naan
Breadsticks, 53
Tempura Shishito Peppers, 60
apples
Apple Fritters, 30
Orange-Glazed Duck Breast with
Apples, 95
asparagus
Asparagus and Goat Cheese Frittata,
25
Prosciutto-Wrapped Asparagus, 58
avocados
Avocado Fries with Pomegranate
Molasses, 64
Baja Fish Tacos, 118
Roasted Garlic Guacamole with
Homemade Tortilla Chips, 50
Sonoran Hot Dogs, 106
Sweet Potato and Farro Grain Bowls
with Creamy Herb Dressing, 78

B

beans
Freeze-and-Fry Sweet Potato and
Black Bean Breakfast Burritos, 26
Sonoran Hot Dogs, 106
beef
Argentinian Beef Empanadas, 100
Country-Fried Steak with Onion
Gravy, 98
Perfect Spice-Rubbed Ribeye for
One (or Two), 102
Sicilian Stuffed Peppers, 103
Sonoran Hot Dogs, 106
bell peppers
Argentinian Beef Empanadas, 100
Confetti Salmon Burgers, 112
Falafel with Israeli Salad, 70
Maryland Crab Cakes with Sriracha
Mayonnaise, 117
Paneer Tikka, 81
Roasted Red Pepper and Feta Salad,
67
Sicilian Stuffed Peppers, 103
Speedy Shakshuka, 24
breakfast and brunch
Apple Fritters, 30
Asparagus and Goat Cheese Frittata,
25
Cinnamon Streusel French Toast, 29
Eggs in a Basket, 28
Freeze-and-Fry Sweet Potato and
Black Bean Breakfast Burritos, 26
Speedy Shakshuka, 24
Strawberries and Cream Baked
Oatmeal, 33
Two-Ingredient Cream Biscuits, 32
broccoli
Loaded Baked Potatoes with Broccoli
and Cheddar Cheese Sauce, 76
Sweet Potato and Farro Grain Bowls
with Creamy Herb Dressing, 78
Teriyaki Salmon and Broccoli, 114
Brussels sprouts: Spicy Maple-Soy
Brussels Sprouts, 62
burgers
Confetti Salmon Burgers, 112
Mushroom Turkey Burgers, 88
burritos: Freeze-and-Fry Sweet Potato
and Black Bean Breakfast Burritos,
26

C

carrots: Crispy Vegetable Spring Rolls,
44–45
cauliflower
Cauliflower Steaks with Tahini Sauce,
74
KFC (Korean Fried Cauliflower), 66
celery
Confetti Salmon Burgers, 112
Maryland Crab Cakes with Sriracha
Mayonnaise, 117
Cheddar cheese
Freeze-and-Fry Sweet Potato and
Black Bean Breakfast Burritos, 26
Loaded Baked Potatoes with Broccoli
and Cheddar Cheese Sauce, 76
Zucchini Rice Fritters, 71
chicken
Buttermilk Fried Chicken and
Waffles, 86–87
Chicken Parmesan, 85
Chinese Takeout Egg Rolls with Soy-
Vinegar Dipping Sauce, 46
General Tso's Chicken, 94
Israeli Chicken Schnitzel, 91
Piri-Piri Chicken Thighs, 90
Tandoori-Style Chicken Skewers, 92
Tropical Glazed Chicken Salad with
Mangoes and Candied Pecans, 84
chickpeas
Falafel with Israeli Salad, 70
Orange and Rosemary Roasted
Chickpeas, 41
chocolate
Chocolate Chip Pan Cookie Sundae,
134
Churros with Chocolate Dipping
Sauce, 126
Profiteroles, 132
cod: Jalea (Peruvian Fried Seafood with
Salsa Criolla), 120
corn: Elotes (Mexican Street Corn), 56
crabmeat
Crab Rangoon, 48
Maryland Crab Cakes with Sriracha
Mayonnaise, 117
cream cheese: Crab Rangoon, 48
cucumbers
Falafel with Israeli Salad, 70
Zucchini, Spinach, and Feta Pancakes
with Tzatziki, 72–73

D

desserts
  Caramelized Peach Shortcakes, 136–137
  Caramelized Pineapple with Mint and Lime, 138
  Chocolate Chip Pan Cookie Sundae, 134
  Chouquettes (French Pastry Puffs), 131
  Churros with Chocolate Dipping Sauce, 126
  Lemon-Lavender Doughnuts, 128–130
  Profiteroles, 132
duck: Orange-Glazed Duck Breast with Apples, 95

E

eggplants
  Eggplant Parmesan, 80
  Smoky Eggplant Dip with Homemade Pita Chips, 52
egg rolls: Chinese Takeout Egg Rolls with Soy-Vinegar Dipping Sauce, 46
eggs
  Apple Fritters, 30
  Argentinian Beef Empanadas, 100
  Asparagus and Goat Cheese Frittata, 25
  Avocado Fries with Pomegranate Molasses, 64
  Bolivian Croquetas (Tuna-Stuffed Quinoa Patties), 122
  Buttermilk Fried Chicken and Waffles, 86–87
  Cauliflower Steaks with Tahini Sauce, 74
  Chicken Parmesan, 85
  Chocolate Chip Pan Cookie Sundae, 134
  Chorizo Scotch Eggs, 37
  Chouquettes (French Pastry Puffs), 131
  Churros with Chocolate Dipping Sauce, 126
  Cinnamon Streusel French Toast, 29
  Confetti Salmon Burgers, 112
  Country-Fried Steak with Onion Gravy, 98
  Eggplant Parmesan, 80
  Eggs in a Basket, 28
  Freeze-and-Fry Sweet Potato and Black Bean Breakfast Burritos, 26

Fried Green Tomatoes with Rémoulade, 54
Fried Pickles with Buttermilk-Herb Ranch Dressing, 42
Fried Shrimp with Sweet Chili Dipping Sauce, 113
Israeli Chicken Schnitzel, 91
Jalea (Peruvian Fried Seafood with Salsa Criolla), 120
Lemon-Lavender Doughnuts, 128–130
Maryland Crab Cakes with Sriracha Mayonnaise, 117
Monte Cristo Sandwich, 108
Pecan-Crusted Tilapia, 116
Profiteroles, 132
Speedy Shakshuka, 24
Strawberries and Cream Baked Oatmeal, 33
Supplì al Telefono (Roman Rice Croquettes), 38–40
Zucchini Rice Fritters, 71
Zucchini, Spinach, and Feta Pancakes with Tzatziki, 72–73
empanadas
  Argentinian Beef Empanadas, 100
  Kale and Mushroom Empanadas, 75

F

falafel: Falafel with Israeli Salad, 70
farro: Sweet Potato and Farro Grain Bowls with Creamy Herb Dressing, 78
feta cheese
  Roasted Red Pepper and Feta Salad, 67
  Zucchini, Spinach, and Feta Pancakes with Tzatziki, 72–73
fries
  Avocado Fries with Pomegranate Molasses, 64
  Caribbean Yuca Fries, 59
frittatas: Asparagus and Goat Cheese Frittata, 25

G

goat cheese: Asparagus and Goat Cheese Frittata, 25
Gruyère cheese
  Monte Cristo Sandwich, 108
  Zucchini Rice Fritters, 71
guacamole
  Freeze-and-Fry Sweet Potato and Black Bean Breakfast Burritos, 26

Potato and Cheese Taquitos, 36
Roasted Garlic Guacamole with Homemade Tortilla Chips, 50
gyoza: Pork and Cabbage Gyoza, 47

H

ham: Monte Cristo Sandwich, 108

K

kale: Kale and Mushroom Empanadas, 75

L

lamb: Lamb Kofta with Tzatziki, 101

M

mangoes: Tropical Glazed Chicken Salad with Mangoes and Candied Pecans, 84
maple syrup
  Buttermilk Fried Chicken and Waffles, 86–87
  Cinnamon Streusel French Toast, 29
  Spicy Maple-Soy Brussels Sprouts, 62
Mexican cheese
  Elotes (Mexican Street Corn), 56
  Potato and Cheese Taquitos, 36
Mexican crema
  Baja Fish Tacos, 118
  Elotes (Mexican Street Corn), 56
  Sonoran Hot Dogs, 106
mozzarella cheese
  Chicken Parmesan, 85
  Eggplant Parmesan, 80
  Sicilian Stuffed Peppers, 103
  Supplì al Telefono (Roman Rice Croquettes), 38–40
mushrooms
  Chinese Takeout Egg Rolls with Soy-Vinegar Dipping Sauce, 46
  Crispy Vegetable Spring Rolls, 44–45
  Kale and Mushroom Empanadas, 75
  Mushroom Turkey Burgers, 88

O

oats: Strawberries and Cream Baked Oatmeal, 33
oranges
  Orange and Rosemary Roasted Chickpeas, 41
  Orange-Glazed Duck Breast with Apples, 95

P

paneer: Paneer Tikka, 81

Parmesan cheese
  Chicken Parmesan, 85
  Eggplant Parmesan, 80
  Supplì al Telefono (Roman Rice
    Croquettes), 38–40
peaches
  Caramelized Peach Shortcakes,
    136–137
  Tropical Glazed Chicken Salad with
    Mangoes and Candied Pecans, 84
pecans
  Pecan-Crusted Tilapia, 116
  Tropical Glazed Chicken Salad with
    Mangoes and Candied Pecans, 84
pickles: Fried Pickles with Buttermilk-
  Herb Ranch Dressing, 42
pineapple: Caramelized Pineapple with
  Mint and Lime, 138
pork
  Chinese Takeout Egg Rolls with Soy-
    Vinegar Dipping Sauce, 46
  Chorizo Scotch Eggs, 37
  Cumin-Crusted Pork Tenderloin and
    Potatoes, 104
  Monte Cristo Sandwich, 108
  Pork and Cabbage Gyoza, 47
  Sonoran Hot Dogs, 106
  Teriyaki-Glazed Baby Back Ribs, 107
potatoes
  Cumin-Crusted Pork Tenderloin and
    Potatoes, 104
  Loaded Baked Potatoes with Broccoli
    and Cheddar Cheese Sauce, 76
  Potato and Cheese Taquitos, 36
prosciutto: Prosciutto-Wrapped
  Asparagus, 58

Q
quinoa: Bolivian Croquetas (Tuna-
  Stuffed Quinoa Patties), 122

R
rice
  Sicilian Stuffed Peppers, 103
  Supplì al Telefono (Roman Rice
    Croquettes), 38–40
  Zucchini Rice Fritters, 71

S
salads
  Falafel with Israeli Salad, 70

Jalea (Peruvian Fried Seafood with
  Salsa Criolla), 120
Roasted Red Pepper and Feta Salad,
  67
Tropical Glazed Chicken Salad with
  Mangoes and Candied Pecans, 84
salmon
  Confetti Salmon Burgers, 112
  Teriyaki Salmon and Broccoli, 114
salsa
  Baja Fish Tacos, 118
  Freeze-and-Fry Sweet Potato and
    Black Bean Breakfast Burritos, 26
  Jalea (Peruvian Fried Seafood with
    Salsa Criolla), 120
sandwiches: Monte Cristo Sandwich,
  108
shakshuka: Speedy Shakshuka, 24
shrimp
  Fried Shrimp with Sweet Chili
    Dipping Sauce, 113
  Jalea (Peruvian Fried Seafood with
    Salsa Criolla), 120
  Shrimp DeJonghe Skewers, 123
spring rolls: Crispy Vegetable Spring
  Rolls, 44–45
strawberries: Strawberries and Cream
  Baked Oatmeal, 33
sweet potatoes
  Freeze-and-Fry Sweet Potato and
    Black Bean Breakfast Burritos, 26
  Sweet Potato and Farro Grain Bowls
    with Creamy Herb Dressing, 78
Swiss cheese
  Monte Cristo Sandwich, 108
  Zucchini Rice Fritters, 71

T
tacos: Baja Fish Tacos, 118
taquitos: Potato and Cheese Taquitos,
  36
tilapia
  Baja Fish Tacos, 118
  Pecan-Crusted Tilapia, 116
tomatoes
Eggplant Parmesan, 80
  Fried Green Tomatoes with
    Rëmoulade, 54
  Jalea (Peruvian Fried Seafood with
    Salsa Criolla), 120

Roasted Garlic Guacamole with
  Homemade Tortilla Chips, 50
Sicilian Stuffed Peppers, 103
Sonoran Hot Dogs, 106
Speedy Shakshuka, 24
Supplì al Telefono (Roman Rice
  Croquettes), 38–40
tuna: Bolivian Croquetas (Tuna-Stuffed
  Quinoa Patties), 122
turkey
  Monte Cristo Sandwich, 108
  Mushroom Turkey Burgers, 88

V
vegetarian main courses
  Cauliflower Steaks with Tahini Sauce,
    74
  Eggplant Parmesan, 80
  Falafel with Israeli Salad, 70
  Kale and Mushroom Empanadas, 75
  Loaded Baked Potatoes with Broccoli
    and Cheddar Cheese Sauce, 76
  Sweet Potato and Farro Grain Bowls
    with Creamy Herb Dressing, 78
  Zucchini Rice Fritters, 71
  Zucchini, Spinach, and Feta Pancakes
    with Tzatziki, 72–73

Y
yogurt
  Paneer Tikka, 81
  Sweet Potato and Farro Grain Bowls
    with Creamy Herb Dressing, 78
  Tandoori-Style Chicken Skewers, 92
  Tandoori Yogurt Dip with Naan
    Breadsticks, 53
  Zucchini, Spinach, and Feta Pancakes
    with Tzatziki, 72–73
yuca roots: Caribbean Yuca Fries, 59

Z
zucchini
  Zucchini Rice Fritters, 71
  Zucchini, Spinach, and Feta Pancakes
    with Tzatziki, 72–73

CPSIA information can be obtained
at www.ICGtesting.com
Printed in the USA
LVHW051639130223
739098LV00006B/6